Cynicism and Hope

Cynicism and Hope

Reclaiming Discipleship in a
Postdemocratic Society

edited by Meg E. Cox

CASCADE *Books* · Eugene, Oregon

CYNICISM AND HOPE
Reclaiming Discipleship in a Postdemocratic Society

Cascade Books
A Division of Wipf and Stock Publishers
199 W. 8th Ave., Suite 3
Eugene, OR 97401

www.wipfandstock.com

ISBN 13: 978-1-60608-214-0

Cataloging-in-Publication data:

Cynicism and hope : reclaiming discipleship in a postdemocractic society / edited by Meg E. Cox.

xiv + 122 p. ; 23 cm. —Includes bibliographical references.

ISBN 13: 978-1-60608-214-0

1. Hope—Religious aspects—Christianity. 2. Cynicism—social aspects. 3. Christianity and culture. 4. Christianity and politics. I. Cox, Meg E. II. Title.

BR115. P7 C95 2009

Manufactured in the U.S.A.

In memory of

Ted Eatmon

You are glass,
beyond you shines God
—Ruth Goring

Contents

Contents

Preface

It seems strange to be editing a book with *postdemocratic* in the title during what feels like the most democratic presidential campaign in a long while.

Commenting on the name of the conference that inspired this volume, contributor Dale Suderman points out that the word *postdemocratic* wrongly assumes that there once was a time when U.S. society was democratic in the ways we wish it were now. In reality the United States, as most nations, has always been ruled by the people who command the most financial resources. On the other hand, even in the present difficult times we enjoy a society that is far more democratic than many others—as recent developments in Zimbabwe remind us.

Still, the word *postdemocratic* remains useful because it conveys a sense that something important has been lost. Whereas nonviolent direct action produced major changes in U.S. law and society in the 1950s and '60s, the activists who organized the Cynicism and Hope conference in 2007 understood that their activism was unlikely to provoke an end to the Iraq war. Confidence that election results reflect the voters' will is at a low ebb, and elections are more money-driven than ever.

We hope, of course, that the 2008 election season brings about a restoration of what has been lost and the possibility of gaining what never was before, but a healthy cynicism tells us that even the best we can hope for from politics will not be enough. Whoever wins the presidency will be commander in chief of the most powerful killing machine in history; whoever prevails in the congressional elections will be bound by the necessities of politics. Elections are important, but their results are finite.

The gospel is about so much more than the people who win elections and the policies they enact. It is true at all times and in all places. It is true when our leaders choose policies that affirm human life and protect God's creation, and it is true when oilfields are burning and genocide wipes out whole communities. The people who first heard the message of God's kingdom and prayed for it to come on earth were living under the oppressive rule of an imperialistic power, but they would not realize God's kingdom by taking up the sword or voting their oppressors out of office. Rather, they prayed and broke bread together; they shared their goods and loved their enemies and welcomed their neighbors who had been cast aside. They were a foretaste of the kingdom for which they hoped.

~

I thank the Cynicism and Hope team and all of the contributors to this volume for reminding me where to find hope in these dark times. Ruth Goring and Kelley Johnson helped start the project on its way. Each of the contributors was marvelously cooperative whether I requested a few minor edits or a completely new essay. Don Seiden and Amy Davis of the Writers Workspace helped me to find the physical, mental, and spiritual space to imagine this volume, propose it, and pull together all the pieces. Richard Benjamin and Charletta Erb contributed transcription, and Charletta, Tim Nafziger, and Patty Peebles helped me wrap my mind around the introduction. Copy editor Halden Doerge made valuable suggestions and swept up behind me when I got sloppy. My cheerleader and husband, Sean, tolerated more late nights of editing, and our daughters, Mandy and Mackenzie, sacrificed a trip to Camp Menno Haven's rally day so I could get the manuscript in on time.

Most of all, I thank the congregations at Reba Place Church in Evanston, Illinois, and Living Water Community Church in the Rogers Park neighborhood of Chicago—and especially the elder members of both communities. You attract and inspire folks who dream up events like the Cynicism and Hope conference, and you model for us every day how to be a kingdom kind of people.

Peter Dula, whose address inspired the conference, advised his listeners to practice resistance by riding a bike and planting a garden. Well, Peter, my tires are full, and tonight we enjoyed the first produce of our new garden.

Meg E. Cox
July 2008

Introduction

by Meg E. Cox

On the weekend of November 3, 2007, two hundred people gathered at Reba Place Church in Evanston, Illinois, for a conference called Cynicism and Hope: Reclaiming Discipleship in a Postdemocratic Society. The event was organized by a group of mostly twenty-something Mennonites from Reba Place and its daughter congregation, Living Water Community Church in the Rogers Park neighborhood of Chicago.

The idea for the conference had emerged from discussions about a speech by Peter Dula, the former Mennonite Central Committee coordinator for Iraq, on the morning after the March 2007 Christian Peace Witness for Iraq in Washington, D.C. The previous evening, three thousand people had gathered at the Washington National Cathedral and marched four miles through sleet and freezing rain to hold a prayer vigil outside the White House on the fourth anniversary of the war.

"Peter spoke simply and honestly about the caustic combination of guilt and disempowerment that attacks those of us living in the United States," wrote organizer Tim Nafziger in a Beliefnet article announcing the November conference. "We are complicit in horrific acts of destruction, but our leaders have largely abandoned the rusty apparatus of democracy." Protests had begun to "feel like empty rituals."[1]

After Peter's speech, the group from Reba Place and Living Water climbed back into their van and began the twelve-hour drive home. They learned that each of them had been electrified by what Peter had said. He had finally named aloud what Tim and his companions had been struggling with. "Those of us who have come of age in the Bush administration," Tim wrote, "remain caught beneath a crust of cynicism that permeates every corner of our mental and spiritual space."

As the group discussed their need to "talk honestly about our disillusionment and learn from our failure and that of those who have gone before us," Tim continued, "a surprisingly concrete idea emerged. We wanted to invite Peter and others to Chicago to continue the conversation." The conference they envisioned would address three questions:

How do we live out God's call to prophetic witness in an apathetic and disempowered society?

How can we learn from others who have remained faithful to Jesus' radical call in the midst of failure?

How can art, prayer, and other forms of everyday resistance nourish our hope for the kingdom of God?

The two hundred who responded to the invitation heard from church leaders and academics, social-service providers and leaders of intentional communities. Some of these addresses (or essays based on the addresses) are collected here. The arts also figured prominently in the event. After the closing liturgy, attenders enjoyed a dance choreographed for the conference, and Ruth Goring, an editor and freelance writer, read a poem she had written for the occasion.

A week after the Cynicism and Hope conference, Ruth presented her poem during Sunday worship at Living Water Church. Afterwards, conference committee member Kelley Johnson testified to the congregation that she had been worn down by the anger that was the prevailing emotion among her activist friends. Ruth's poem gave her hope; it suggested a new way to live within what Kelley called the "uncomfortable, layered tension" between the hope that things will get better and cynicism about whether they ever will.

1. Nafziger, "Cynicism."

Like the demonstrators in Washington, many Christian activists in the United States have suffered despair, have felt paralyzed, have needed comfort. When we invest our hope in expectations of large-scale, structural change, Kelley said, "we easily fall into bitterness," but the conference "offered the alternative of finding hope in small, everyday actions" and created a "place for lament that tempers misplaced hope and the idealism that we often use to counter our bitterness." At the November gathering, people for whom activism had become an idol learned that it's "OK to be a good neighbor and parent," Kelley said, that living with radical Christian faithfulness in our neighborhoods and congregations can itself be a profoundly hopeful political act.

In the months following the conference, we at Living Water encountered new opportunities to act out this radical faithfulness. A large number of neighborhood children became regular guests at our midweek potluck dinner; a group of Burundian families recently arrived in the United States from a refugee camp in Tanzania decided to make Living Water their church home; and the congregation accompanied our brother Ted Eatmon through his final months until he died of lung cancer at home in the middle of an April night, surrounded by people from his church family.

After Ted died, I asked Living Water member Patty Peebles, a hospice nurse who had organized the congregation's care for him, what it was like to be trained to heal people's bodies, then care for patients who are sure to die. She said that hospice is also about healing, but healing of the mind and spirit—for both the patient and the patient's loved ones.

If we had gathered around Ted merely to pray for his physical healing, in protest of his decline, we would have been far more despairing in his death. But we accepted his departure as inevitable and walked through it with him and with his family. We would not have been able to do this gracefully if we didn't acknowledge that his body was broken and needed to die.

The March 2007 demonstration in Washington was called a peace witness, not an antiwar protest. Believing that the demonstration would end the war was a recipe for paralyzing despair. Knowing that the war would continue and demonstrating nonetheless, then going home to live toward the kingdom of God suggests a more hopeful way.

Cynicism, Hope, Discipleship, and Democracy

An Invitation

by Tim Nafziger

How do we live out God's call to prophetic witness in an apathetic and disempowered society? How can we learn from others who have remained faithful to Jesus' radical call in the midst of failure?

These don't sound like the questions you'd expect to be hearing from a van full of exhausted young adults on a twelve-hour drive back to Chicago from Washington, D.C.

But last March, that's exactly what happened to a group of us from Living Water Community Church in Chicago and Reba Place Church in Evanston, Illinois, on our way back from the Christian Peace Witness for Iraq.

Our epiphany did not take place at the Washington National Cathedral or during the bone-numbing walk to the White House. Instead, it happened the following morning during a humble gathering of Mennonites in the basement of a Methodist church lit by fluorescent lights and filled with orange and red plastic chairs. We were eating bagels and drinking juice and

---

This is a reprint (with very minor modifications) of a September 2007 Beliefnet article inviting people to the November 2007 Cynicism and Hope conference. The dates mentioned herein reflect that original publication.

listening to Peter Dula, the Mennonite Central Committee coordinator for Iraq from 2004 to 2006.

Peter spoke simply and honestly about the caustic combination of guilt and disempowerment that attacks those of us living in the United States. We are complicit in horrific acts of destruction, but our leaders have largely abandoned the rusty apparatus of democracy—a trend accelerated by Bush and company. Our protests begin to feel like empty rituals. Politicians have taken advantage of our culture's apathy and nihilism to shed the last vestiges of accountability. As Peter put it, "We are no longer enough of a democracy that the people feel empowered, but still enough of one that people feel responsible."

We left D.C. immediately after Peter's talk and discovered that each of us in the van had been electrified by what he had said. Those of us who have come of age during the Bush administration live with the knowledge that something is deeply wrong with our country, but we remain caught beneath a crust of cynicism that permeates every corner of our mental and spiritual space.

On the van ride home to Chicago we talked about how important it is for our generation to talk honestly about our disillusionment and learn from our failure and that of those who have gone before us. As we discussed what to do next, a surprisingly concrete idea emerged. We wanted to invite Peter and others to Chicago to continue the conversation. We even came up with a title for our gathering—Cynicism and Hope: Reclaiming Discipleship in a Postdemocratic Society. I've had epiphanies on protest road trips before, but never with so many people so committed to doing something about it. If you feel the same way, come join us in Chicago on November 2 and 3 (one year before the 2008 elections): www.cynicismandhope.org.

Cynicism and Hope

Address to Participants in the Christian Peace Witness for Iraq, March 2007

by Peter Dula

Talking about Iraq is always difficult. It is difficult because it is sad, because it is complex. It is difficult because the divides that now crisscross that land have become so confusing. But mostly it is difficult because I have this feeling that it doesn't do any good, that everything that needed to be said has been said yet goes unheard in Washington. But I will start with two stories, one about the Americans in Iraq, one about Iraqis.

My first week in Baghdad in January 2004, Edward Miller and Steve Weaver took me to one of Marla Ruzicka's famous parties at the Al Hamra Hotel. There were two young Americans there named Ray and Jeff, though we always called them Mutt and Jeff. Now they are rather famous as Baghdad party animals. They came up in a *Harper's Magazine* article about expat life in Baghdad, and in a Salon.com piece. An episode of NPR's *This American Life* was devoted to them. But that was later. That night at the Al Hamra was their first party in Iraq and mine too. They had also just arrived that week. They were wearing ratty jeans and T-shirts of punk bands. Ray had on a Boston Red Sox cap. They had made quite a bit of money in Boston selling T-shirts at Fenway emblazoned with two words in oversized block letters: "Yankees Suck."

They had jobs at the nongovernment-organization (NGO) assistance office in the Green Zone, and when Marla introduced us and they realized that Mennonite Central Committee (MCC) did some work with local NGOs, they got excited. "We can work together," they said. "What's your plan? You got a plan?" They, like me, had been in Iraq just a week. As they kept pushing for our plan to "get this country going again, get these people back on their feet," we mumbled MCC platitudes about patience—drinking tea, studying Arabic, listening. It takes time, we said. Ray responded, "Not if we hustle." By this point they had dispensed with wine glasses and were swigging straight from the bottles on the table. When we left, Ray embraced Steve and whispered in his ear, "Let's fix this shit."

The episode of *This American Life* tries to move the listener from laughter to tears. Ray and Jeff joke about how they were drinking on the bus ride across the desert from Jordan to Baghdad. This would have been hugely offensive to the vast majority of the Muslims they were riding with, but perhaps they were just unaware of that aspect of Islamic culture. They end by telling the story of the death of a close Iraqi co-worker, killed, most likely, because he worked with the Americans. And so it was actually a quite brilliant little summary of the occupation. The Americans ride in drunk and ignorant and end up killing the ones they came to help without even trying.[1]

For some people, I suppose, the image of the troops pulling down the statue of Saddam remains the most indelible image of the early days of the occupation. For me the most indelible image is that of those two brash, enthusiastic, foolish young men. They had access to resources, to power, and to Green Zone committees. They were one way to get things done in Iraq.

Here is another way.

No one knows how old Sr. Teresa is, but they know from the convent records that she joined the monastery in 1922. That puts her at about a hundred, give or take a couple years. She is bent and shrunken and reminds me of Yoda. By now she is quite senile. Last time I was at the convent she greeted me by reaching up and pulling my face down to her, laying her cheek against mine. They told her I was a priest from America, and she said, "No, he is from Mangesh," the village where I first met her six months earlier.

I am not a priest, but the other sisters seem to think that she will be more comfortable with me staying there if she thinks I am. She is not so senile as to believe it. Sometimes when she spots me, she hides the Sacred Heart hanging from her neck, swinging it around so it hangs down her

---

1. *This American Life*, "My Big Break."

back, hidden by her veil. She says I must be one of Sr. Basma's friends. "She likes Protestants." I take it this means that Sr. Basma was friendlier with the troops last year than Sr. Teresa thought they deserved. "Protestants are human beings too," Sr. Basma says. Sr. Teresa brushes her off with a wave of her hand and then dozes off at the lunch table.

One of the main tasks of the younger sisters is caring for Sr. Teresa. They take turns fanning her when it is warm, which is most of the time. They also take turns sleeping with her. When she dozed off at lunch Sr. Maria explained, "She does not sleep well at night since Sr. Cecille died." Sr. Cecille was murdered in the Baghdad convent shortly after midnight August 15, 2002. She was seventy-one. It had been just Sr. Cecille and Sr. Maria living there. Sr. Maria had left the day before to travel north for the Feast. She returned the next day to find Cecille stripped of her clothes, tied to a bed full of blood. She had been stabbed multiple times. They don't know who killed her. "Maybe Saddam, maybe Wahhabis, maybe Syrians, who knows?" said Sr. Maria.

She told me, "I don't know where I got the strength that day. And I don't know why I have survived, why I happened to be absent the night they killed Sr. Cecille. I think there must be a reason, don't you?" I expected her to go on to say something pious like, "God preserved me for the work I am doing now." But when she continued, she said that she feared that something still more horrible than that event was coming, something that she would not survive.

I call Sr. Maria every now and then. Back in November some old friends in Oregon who were trying to find a way to connect to Iraq recalled the sisters I had written about and wanted to send them some money. I called Sr. Maria to get her banking information so we could make a transfer. She was almost entirely uninterested. But what she said, at least a dozen times in the ten-minute phone call, was "Pray for us. Pray for Iraq. Pray for me."

I realize that that might not seem like much of an answer to the question, What can we do about Iraq? But it moves us toward one of the most important things I want to say this morning. I don't think I am alone when I say that when I come to Washington, or write a letter to a congressperson, or march in a protest, I feel like an atheist at prayer. I have no more hope that those actions are heard or seen than an atheist does that her prayer gets past the ceiling.

So the question I want to address this morning is not, What should we do? Or, What should we say? Or, How do we advocate? We might get there, but asking those questions too quickly can be very misleading. The first question, the one I want to spend most of my time with is, Why are those questions so hard to answer these days? To put it another way, I want to stop and tarry with, linger with, this feeling I am guessing most of us in this room share. What is that feeling?

It is a sense of both helplessness and guilt. A sense that nothing we can do or say will make a difference, combined with a feeling of complicity. Somehow it is our fault. One way to say it is that we are no longer enough of a democracy that the people feel empowered, but still enough of one that people feel responsible. In other words, Bush has done to democracy what Calvin did to God. That suggests another aspect of the feeling: a disgust with our fellow Americans for allowing that to happen. If we blame ourselves, we have to blame them. It isn't about pointing fingers at red-staters. This was, after all, a liberal's war. Bill Clinton signed the Iraq Liberation Act in 1998 committing the United States to a policy of regime change. Almost all the Democrats in Congress voted for the invasion of Iraq even in the presence of the alternative bill that did not oppose the invasion but merely insisted on waiting on the UN. Even those unaffected by the political pressures those Democrats faced, the so-called liberal-humanitarians such as Michael Ignatieff, also were active and articulate promoters of the invasion.

So that is the feeling. Where does it come from? There are at least two parts to an answer to that question. One is about Iraq, and the other is about the post-9/11 United States, but of course they go together. I am going to pay relatively little attention to the first one, Iraq. What is there to say anymore? All the facts are out there. Most people who read the papers have no trouble reciting the mistakes: the Pentagon's refusal to listen to the State Department or the army chiefs of staff; the failure to properly review the intelligence on weapons of mass destruction; the abandonment of the Future of Iraq project; the Coalition Provisional Authority's cronyism in hiring; the decision to disband the Iraqi army; debaathification; the over-reliance on Iraqi exiles who hadn't set foot in Iraq in thirty-five years; the decision to keep the UN at arm's length until too late.

But for the last year and a half there have been a new set of issues, revolving around increasing sectarian violence. The NGO community in Amman started to become fully aware in the summer of 2005 just how wide the division between Sunni and Shi'a was becoming. In June 2005, Steve Fainaru and Anthony Shadid, perhaps the finest journalists report-ing from Iraq, wrote in the *Washington Post* that Arab prisoners were being transported to prisons in the north, where they were guarded by

Kurds.[2] Later that summer a close friend of mine, an Iraqi staff member of a European NGO, was arrested and imprisoned. When he was released a few weeks later, he told us that in his prison almost all the guards were Shi'a and almost all the prisoners Sunni. Such activities seemed to us careless at best. U.S. policy was supposed to be minimizing sectarian differences, not exacerbating them. Any hope for that was shattered in February 2006 when the Askariya Mosque in Samarra, one of Shi'a Islam's holiest shrines, was bombed. Some have called that the beginning of the Iraqi civil war. Since then the fact of ethnic cleansing in Iraq has become unmistakable.

Trying to settle on a date for when the civil war began, however, is a fruitless exercise. The crucial thing is to connect the dots between the current sectarian violence and the occupation's early mistakes, for the roots of the problem go back to the very beginning, to George Bush's fateful decision to disband the Iraqi army. That decision meant that three hundred thousand Iraqi men with machine guns were not just unemployed, but frustrated, discontented, and ripe for recruitment by criminal gangs and a growing movement to destabilize the occupation. It also meant that the United States would need to create an Iraqi army from scratch. But either because the task was too difficult or the resources too few, progress was minimal. As security in Iraq steadily declined, the United States turned to already-existing militias such as the Kurdish *peshmergas* and the Iranian-trained Shi'a Badr Brigade.

In other words, what was supposed to be the solution is now the problem. The militias to which the United States turned have created an Iraq riven by sectarian violence and have made its central government an illusion. This state of affairs brings up disturbing memories of Iraqi history: before Saddam's Baath party took power, Iraq had never had a government strong enough to control the military. We keep digging. And the hole keeps getting deeper.

So that is the first part. The second is what has happened here at home. Something has happened, or has seemed to happen, to politics in America. It is impossible to give a full account of this story in this space. It has to do in part with the rise of global capitalism, which has meant that fewer and fewer corners of the globe and of our souls are uncolonized by the market. Every form of resistance is now co-opted (as Walmart's recent turn to organic demonstrates), and more and more obstacles to corporate power crumble. It has to do with 9/11 and the creation and exploitation of

2. Fainaru and Shadid, "Kurdish Officials."

a climate of fear. It has to do with the Bush administration and its capacity for mendacity. But the picture of Dick Cheney and Donald Rumsfeld in the Oval Office with Gerald Ford that was frequently published after Ford's death reminds us that Bush was no innovator.

Perhaps one way to describe our situation is to say that there has been, over the last several decades, an increasing apathy among the citizenry. We have witnessed the decline of what little was left of an ethos of democratic participation and responsibility. Yet to say only that would be misleading. American political lethargy is hardly new. Alexis de Tocqueville spotted it already 175 years ago. So two qualifications are necessary. First, it is not our current apathy that is anomalous, but the surge of democratic energies around civil rights, feminism and Vietnam to which we are prone to compare ourselves. Second, what has changed in the last six years is the way our political elites deal with the popular inaction.

Any attrition of democratic possibility in government has always kept pace with popular cynicism, but this administration was able to accelerate attrition by taking advantage of it to an unprecedented degree. They spotted it and made exploiting it the key to the most extraordinary expansion of state power in U.S. history since the New Deal. They didn't even pay lip service to the popular will as previous administrations did, because they realized that they didn't have to. They realized that most of us, or enough of us, were either supportive or too cynical, apathetic, or depressed to care. A 2003 *Harper's Magazine* article said that we live under a "new censorship," the genius of which is that it works through "the obscenity of absolute openness."[3]

We know that the U.S. government is in the pockets of the corporations. We know that our homes and phones are no longer immune from government intrusion. We know that our government is actively and unrepentantly torturing prisoners of war even after Abu Ghraib with congressional and public approval. We know that in order to do that Bush invented a category called "unlawful enemy combatants," a category the likes of which has not been seen since the Third Reich. We know that this administration has invented a whole new type of extraordinary rendition. We know that we have turned Baghdad and much of Iraq into an apocalyptic nightmare that makes Lebanon in the early '80s look safe. We know that many times more people died in Iraq in July than were killed in the entire course of Israel's bombing of Lebanon this summer.

3. White, "New Censorship."

They knew we wouldn't care. They knew you could splatter pictures of Abu Ghraib all over every front-page in the world, follow it up with front-page pictures of Cindy Sheehan camping out in Crawford, Texas, and top it all off with Hurricane Katrina, and still win an election. The 2006 election was not, as many people said, a referendum on the Iraq war or the war on terror. It was a referendum on the failure of those wars. This is a crucial point to make, especially for us pacifists. Diane McWhorter wrote in *Slate* that the message the Republicans got in November was not, "Next time, don't do it," but, "Next time, make it work."[4]

I am trying out loud to get a sense of where we are. I am trying to do so in a way that might explain our feelings of helplessness and guilt as well as account for the unprecedented mendacity of the Bush administration in a manner that acknowledges its continuity with prior developments in American politics. I am trying to recognize the expansions of state power under the Bush administration while not underestimating the difficulty the American people have always had in wresting power from their government. I am trying to acknowledge that a properly historical perspective ought to mitigate despair over the Bush regime. But I also can't help but think that people who say that too quickly really don't care much about Iraq.

So now we finally arrive at the question I postponed at the beginning: What do we do? Let me say at the outset that, contrary to what some people seem to assume, you don't feel any less helpless, guilty and stupid after spending two and a half years as MCC Iraq Program Coordinator.

It seems to me that there are at least two dangers to avoid here, though frankly I have little idea how. The first danger would be to act as if nothing had changed, to act as if it were politics as usual in America or Iraq. Thinking that conventional politics still works plays exactly into the hands of those in power. While they are doing something else, we are maintaining the façade for them, which is exactly what they want. I have heard far too many Iraq conversations in which people seem to think that if only we got the right bunch of smart UN bureaucrats together, we could work out a solution. There is a way of emphasizing the mistakes of this war that leaves the purpose of the war unchallenged. That is, some suggest that because Bush's Pentagon was so incompetent, we can't generalize from this war to future wars run by objective statesmen, not ideological hacks. I want to say that there is no solution to Iraq, and more than that: one can only think there is a solution if they share the Bush administration's illusions about

4. McWhorter, "N-Word."

just what we have done there. The more one thinks it is solvable, the more one misunderstands the magnitude of the catastrophe.

But that said, the second danger would be to use this awareness as a way to deepen or excuse our cynicism. That too, it should be obvious, plays into their hands. There may no longer be such a thing as political voice in this country. But if we are not yet reduced to silence, then there must still remain political sobs, political screams.

Here are three things we can do.

The first and most obvious thing, given the occasion, is to march in Washington. We should be here. And if you were one of those who chose civil disobedience last night, you were right to do so. Not, perhaps, because being here makes a difference to the government, but because it registers our dissent and encourages others to register theirs. "Protest that endures," wrote Wendell Berry, "is moved by a hope far more modest than that of public success: namely, the hope of preserving qualities in one's own heart and spirit that would be destroyed by acquiescence."[5]

Perhaps nothing so clearly registers dissent as war-tax resistance. The cost of the wars in Iraq and Afghanistan are now over $300 billion. In 2003 the War Resisters League predicted, "If the 'war on terrorism' lasts a long time—as President Bush has promised—then there is sure to be an enormous growth in the peace movement with a major resurgence in war tax resistance."[6] That the prediction seems not to have come true may just be more evidence for the depth of American apathy. Or it may be due to the fact that this war, despite its cost, has not included a tax increase.

Finally, given that the war we are protesting is an oil war, resistance will mean finding ways to use less oil. At the least, the answer to What should we do? is something like this: Try to ride your bike or walk for all or most of your short trips. Join a local-food group—most of our food, "organic" or not, comes drenched in diesel—and learn to think of gardening as resistance. It may be a meager and flimsy resistance, but it is a necessary one because in its small way it wrests control from those in power. That is, in a time when we feel like everything is out of our control, reclaiming power over the most basic things, what we put in our mouths, is a requirement. That so many have done so is a sign of hope. That this is what so many feel reduced to, is not.

5. Berry, *What Are People For?* 62.

6. Hedemann and Benn, *War Tax Resistance*, 45.

Three Cheers for Cynicism

by Ric Hudgens

Cynicism is a pervasive reality in our culture and in our church and within our hearts. In *The Simpsons Movie*, Bart says, "This is the worst day of my life." And Homer, being the dad of the year, says, "The worst day . . . so far." We all know that feeling. Things are bad and they are probably going to get worse. And yet somehow we can also laugh at Homer because what he says is part of the truth, even though it is not the whole truth.

We also have an intense desire for hope. We realize that hope is what sustains us. Hope is what keeps us going. Hope is what energizes us, brings us joy, and builds community. We live in an age of misplaced hope, but we can cultivate a well-placed hope by considering the virtues of cynicism— of a constructive sort of cynicism that we need as part of our Christian activism.

My dog died about nine days ago. That is really a wrong way to say it, because we put him to death. He was twelve years old, his hips were decayed, he was having trouble breathing, and he spent most of the night moaning and whining. We finally had to put him down. I am still grieving and I am still amazed at how much I miss that little dog. I cry over him and over every dog I have lost in my entire life. Humans have this weird love for dogs.

Once I was looking at some pictures with my father. Dad seems to have owned a dozen dogs throughout his life. He was a hunter who bought, sold, and traded hunting dogs. As we went through the box of photos I would find a picture of one of those dogs and ask what he remembered about it. "Oh yes, that's old Nelly, I bought for her for fifty dollars. She was a good dog." We would find another picture, "Oh yes, that's old Blue. I had Blue for about three years and he was a great dog."

And then we came across a picture of my dad in the navy. He was sitting on a chair with a quite attractive young woman sitting on his lap. I said, "Dad, who is this woman?" And he looked quizzical and scratched his head and said, "I can't remember her name."

Humans and dogs have had this unique love affair.

One of the great dog lovers of all time lived in the fourth century BC in Greece. His name was Diogenes. Diogenes admired dogs so much that he thought they were a good model for how humanity should live. Diogenes developed an entire philosophy and an entire philosophical school based on the imitation of dogs. He asserted that civilization was too complex and dehumanizing. Civilization was putting too much distance between us and nature.

In order to get back to the animal basics of it all, Diogenes lived a life of voluntary poverty. He slept in a barrel; he wandered the streets, sometimes naked; he did things in public that people normally do only in private. And he argued with the philosophers and the wise people of the day, pointing out the inconsistencies and foolishness of their thinking and living.

The name of the school of philosophy that developed around Diogenes was based on the Greek word for one who barks like a dog. This is the origin of the term *cynicism*. In the ancient days, the Cynics were counter-cultural figures. They were very ascetic, they were provocative and controversial, and they were active in the public square, confronting hypocrisy and speaking truth to power. They sound a lot like the early Anabaptists!

Modern cynicism is a very different thing. It is more of an attitude than a lifestyle. Modern cynicism can be contrasted to naïveté and skepticism. The naive or credulous take things at face value. Whatever anyone happens to assert, they nod their heads and say, "OK." So, if the U.S. government says there are weapons of mass destruction in Iraq, then 80 percent of the people say, "Yes, there must be weapons of mass destruction, because Washington said so." If Washington says that Saddam Hussein was funding Al Qaeda and contributed to 9/11, everybody says that must be the way it is. That sort of credulousness takes whatever is disseminated and never suspects that we are being fed lies.

Skeptics take a different position. Skepticism is a disinclination to take things at face value. The skeptic says, "Wait a minute now. I am not sure that is true. I have a lot questions about that." But still the skeptic weighs and balances it: on the one hand, on the other hand. Most of us value skepticism but are suspicious, or skeptical, of cynicism.

The cynic questions not only the bare assertions that are being made, but also the underlying assumptions that support them. The cynic may even question the motives and character of those who are making the assertions. The cynic questions the presumption of common ground and even the rules of the game. The cynic is seen as a threat to the conversation that the naive and the skeptical are trying to maintain.

Many people consider this kind of cynicism as a problem and a threat to the health of our democratic process. You get quotes from people like Jim Wallis and Michael Lerner and Paul Loeb, who say that the choice of society today is between cynicism and hope. We have to choose one or the other. We have to choose to remain cynical and be suspicious of everything, or we have to choose hope, which is the opposite of that.

Now clearly hope is a good thing. Hope is our ability to trust in the future and know that the things that we are doing today are going to have lasting benefit tomorrow. Hope is essential to human community. Because of hope we can keep investing in love and in caring. We can make sacrifices and delay gratification.

Human beings are so hungry for hope that we will even find hope where there is no good reason to be hopeful. We will put hope in things that we should not put hope in just because we have this hope mechanism inside of us that keeps pushing us to always hope for the best.

Hope brings us joy and love and community. It brings us energy and empowers our activism. When we do not have hope we get paralyzed, we get static, we get stuck. We wonder, What is the use?

Because our hopes are often misplaced, we grow cynical when what we hope for doesn't materialize. Our cynicism fuels our desire for new hope. And we get into a vicious cycle. Our misplaced hope leads to more cynicism, and cynicism leads to more misplaced hope. Many of us at this conference are asking ourselves: Is there any other way to live?

I am going to talk about two things. First of all, I want to parse the title of our conference and see what we can learn from that. And second, I want to talk about how a constructive cynicism can contribute to the formation of a radical Christian hope.

So let's talk about the title of this conference: "Cynicism and Hope: Reclaiming Discipleship in a Postdemocratic Society." What is a post-democratic society? Empirical observation tells us that democracies are struggling. They struggle to begin with, and then they often begin to evolve away from their foundations and turn into aristocracies or plutocracies. Elections no longer mean anything. People vote, but nothing changes. Government is no longer of the people, by the people, for the people. If elected officials are always from a certain social class, with a certain level of education, or members of a certain profession or background, then democracy begins to erode. Citizens' rights are not always respected by the state or by the representatives of the state. Healthy political debate becomes more and more difficult and all you get are politicians standing behind podiums talking about minutiae. That is what we mean by a postdemocratic society. A postdemocratic society has all the pretensions of democracy with very little of the reality. And that is why so many of us are so cynical.

Charles Taylor recently wrote: "The emergence of a world civilization, highly unified economically, politically, and in communications, has exacted, and will go on exacting, a tremendous human cost in the death or near death of cultures. And this will be made worse because those who dominate modern civilization have trouble grasping what the costs involve."[1]

This emerging civilization to which Taylor refers is steeped in myth. We live with the myth that expansive economic growth will solve all the problems of poverty and hunger and disease. We live with the myth that everyone in the world will be able to live at the same level of wealth and prosperity currently available to many (but not all) in the West.

We deny that the overdeveloped West is actually contributing to an increase in poverty, hunger, and disease around the world. We refuse to acknowledge that Western levels of consumption are not sustainable ecologically, economically, or politically. There is no way the world is ever going to live at the level of the West, and there is probably no way the West can continue to live at the levels we have already attained.

What does this feel like to us? What is it like to live in an emerging world civilization held captive by subversive mythologies?

1. Taylor, "Different Kind of Courage."

As we sit here tonight, it seems like things keep getting worse. It seems like there is way too much information. It seems like nobody listens to what we have to say. It seems as if there is nothing anyone can do. We see Washington practicing the politics of cynicism. After 9/11 we see the terrorizing war against terror, the Patriot Act and the reduction of civil rights, stolen elections, closed borders, and increasing xenophobia. And what is offered as an alternative to the politics of cynicism but the politics of misplaced hope?

What does the church have to say in a postdemocratic society? Well, that is where we get to the "reclaiming discipleship" part of our conference title. We are not talking about rediscovering discipleship, as if discipleship has been lost and we simply have to find it again. No, we are talking about reclaiming discipleship. The definition of *reclaiming* is to claim back something that has been taken away, something that has been temporarily given to another. To reclaim discipleship is like converting unusable land, a desert or a marsh, into land that would be suitable for cultivation. We are talking about reclaiming discipleship in a postdemocratic society.

But who are we reclaiming discipleship from? Well, there are many ready answers for that. James Dobson and Pat Robertson are reclaiming discipleship from the secular humanists. Tony Campolo and Chris Hedges are reclaiming discipleship from the religious right. Who or what are we reclaiming discipleship from?

Jim Wallis has been one of the most prominent proponents of the cynicism-or-hope dichotomy that I am questioning. But in a May 1979 article in *Sojourners* magazine, Wallis provided what I think is the best answer to the question of who are we reclaiming discipleship from. I go back to this article at least once a year because I think it is one of the best things Wallis ever wrote. It's called "Idols Closer to Home." In this article, Wallis pointed out the cynicism in society. He described the tendency toward false idolatry that we saw manifested in society, but then he held up a mirror to those of us who were sure that we saw through all that.

Wallis talked about idols that are much closer to home. Idols served by those of us who think we understand what radical discipleship really means—those of us committed to simple living, to nonviolence, to speaking truth to power. Such idols are perhaps hidden inside the backpacks of people who come to conferences about radical discipleship in postdemocratic societies.

Wallis talked about how we trust these idols and forget about the grace of God and the power of the Holy Spirit. We become so impressed with ourselves and our ability to speak truths that no one else is speaking—or even perceiving. We reject the prestige of the world only to seek the prestige of our own radical status. In that article Wallis leaves us with the thought that we need to reclaim discipleship from ourselves. We need to reclaim discipleship from the idols that those of us here in this room worship. The idols that continually threaten to contain our faith and hold it captive. If during this weekend together we can take some steps toward seeing our own captivity, then there is some hope that we might be able to contribute to the freedom of others.

Hope or cynicism is a false dichotomy. There are two types of hope. There is misplaced hope that breeds destructive cynicism. And there is a radical hope that carries us out of the vicious cycle of promiscuous idolatry and into the freedom of a reclaimed discipleship. A radical Christian hope looks to God as its source and sustainer.

Cynicism, it is said, is the result of having too much knowledge. We know too much about the world; we know too much about the evils in the world. With all this knowledge, how can we help but be cynical? But from a Christian standpoint, our cynicism is a result of too little knowledge. We are cynical because we do not have the big picture of who God is and what God is about in the world.

There is a destructive cynicism that is the opposite of simple hope. This is the cynicism that arises from repeatedly unmet expectations and false hopes that leave us disillusioned and ultimately paralyzed. But I want to talk to you about the constructive cynicism that is a foundational element of radical hope. We need constructive cynicism as one of the weapons of the Spirit so we can escape the vicious cycle of misplaced hope.

This alliance of cynicism and hope should not be surprising. There are obvious parallels between the early church and the Greek Cynics represented by Diogenes and his followers. If someone in Roman society had observed the early church without an awareness of its Jewish context, they might have supposed they were observing a school of Cynics.

Jesus' own lifestyle was not dissimilar to that of Diogenes. He wandered around from place to place. He lived off the charity of others. He spoke truth to power. He did things that he was not supposed to do. Several scholars, such as John Dominic Crossan and Burton Mack, have asserted that Jesus was little more than a wandering Jewish Cynic. Although I disagree with Crossan and Mack, the parallels between Jesus, the early church, and Greek Cynicism are intriguing.

Similarly intriguing are the parallels with the Hebrew prophets. People like Amos and Jeremiah lived simply, were trying to get back to the foundations, were speaking truth to power, and were suffering for it. These Hebrew prophets are famous for speaking out about the types of social justice issues you and I get passionate about. The prophets would have perhaps been attracted to a conference like this—with all our cynicism and our hope, with all our dismay and outrage at the state of the world, the suffering of the poor.

But the prophets would have gone one step farther than we usually do. The prophets would have pointed us to a source for the injustices that we decry. The prophets would have wanted to talk about idolatry.

Idolatry is an anachronistic topic in our day. We do not see people bowing down to statues and staging human sacrifices today. Yet idolatry was very much a reality within Israel and Judah, and it was to idolatry that the Hebrew prophets linked the reality of injustice. For the prophets the injustice happening to the poor was rooted in one of two forms of idolatry: either believing in false gods or falsely worshiping the one true God.

Idol making seems to be a constant human predisposition or tendency. We like to worship things. We like to make them the center of our lives. We like to make almost anything the center of our lives except God, who should be the center of our lives. We hunger for idols in the same way that we hunger for hope: we worship things, obey them, follow them, and sacrifice for them just as if they were gods. We have misplaced hope in false gods.

In moving to a radical hope, we must criticize misplaced hope. And in order to criticize misplaced hope we must employ the same constructive cynicism to which the Hebrew prophets gave voice. Unmasking idols is one of the first steps in the cultivation of the type of hope that we need. We have to become aware of the idols that we obey and that hold us captive. Constructive cynicism clears the ground of idols and turns the soil, making the cultivation of radical hope possible.

The Apostle Paul was getting at radical hope when he spoke in Romans 4 about "hope against hope." This radical hope may look a lot like Greek Cynicism. It will be countercultural. It will be ascetic. It will be provocative and public. It will name idolatry. It will be sustainable for the long haul. Radical hope will form radical Christian communities because none of us are strong enough to stand alone; the mission of God is all about forming communities of hope. Radical hope will call us to doxology, true worship of the one true God.

I got the phrase *radical hope* from a book by Jonathan Lear on the Crow Indians titled *Radical Hope: Ethics in the Face of Cultural Devastation*. Lear tells the story of the Crow Nation at the turn of the century and of their chief Plenty Coups. A biographer was interviewing Plenty Coups, who was talking about his great feats as a warrior and about the life of his people on the plains. Toward the end of the interview Plenty Coups said, "When the buffalo went away, the hearts of my people fell to the ground and they could not lift them up again, and after this nothing happened."[2]

It was the phrase "after this nothing happened" that set Lear's mind and heart on fire. What did Plenty Coups mean by that? After the buffalo were gone, "the hearts of my people fell to the ground and they could not lift them up again." Their very way of life came to an end, a way of life that was centered and built around the buffalo. Their hearts fell. They could not lift them up again, and after that, Plenty Coups said thirty years later, nothing happened. It was precisely this point of a people faced with the end of their way of life that prompted Lear's inquiry. In Lear's view, the chief's story raises a profound ethical question, one that transcends his own time and challenges all of us who are here at this conference: How should we face the possibility that our own culture might collapse?

I do not have to rehearse for you all the reasons we might think our culture could be coming to an end: ecological reasons, political reasons, economic reasons, social reasons. This is a vulnerability that affects each one of us. Insofar as we are inhabitants of an emerging world civilization, and civilizations are vulnerable to historical forces, how do we live with this kind of vulnerability? How do we make sense of facing up to such a challenge courageously?

In the story Lear tells, there is hope. He calls it radical hope. "What makes this hope radical," he writes, "is that it is directed toward a future goodness that transcends the current ability to understand what it is. Radical hope anticipates a good for which those who have the hope as yet lack the appropriate concepts with which to understand it."[3]

2. Lear, *Radical Hope*, 2.

3. Ibid., 103.

Plenty Coups the chief had a dream about a chickadee. The chickadee was an iconic bird within the Crow tradition. From this dream, Plenty Coups took the lesson that the Crow people would survive by imitating the chickadee. The chickadee adapted to whatever conditions it happened to be in, and therefore the Crow people would be able to adapt to the changes in their civilization. They would be able to adapt and survive. They did not need to pick up the weapons that Sitting Bull and the Sioux were picking up in their war against the white conquerors.

This was a radical hope, one for which the Crow had no evidence except this aging chief's dream about a chickadee. What makes this hope radical, Lear writes, is that it is hope "directed toward a future goodness that transcends the current ability to understand what it is." Radical hope anticipates a good for which those who have the hope do not yet have the appropriate concepts to even understand it, and yet they know it is there.

On the basis of these thoughts about cynicism and hope I want to conclude with a caution and an invitation. We need to be wary of our hoping. We need to be wary of our insatiable hunger for hope. We need to be cautious about misplaced hope. We wait for something that we can barely envision or even describe—the reign of God. And perhaps this is where the role of the arts becomes so crucial because artists can try to express those longings and those desires. They can try to give some materiality to the hopes and the dreams that theologians and preachers do not have the words for.

We wait in the darkness and in not knowing, and this is how we can begin to find knowledge and truth. We may not find the answers to our cynicism during this weekend together. We may not find the roots of a new activism. We may not change the wind or mount a new social movement. Maybe we are not called to. Maybe we are called to wait, listen, worship, and pray.

I believe the path of radical hope is the only path that there is. It is the hope against hope of Romans 4, and it is the hope that Paul speaks of in Romans 5:5, the hope that "does not disappoint us, because God's love has been poured into our hearts through the Holy Spirit that has been given to us." Amen.

4

We Wait for Hope

by Nancy Elizabeth Bedford

While I was preparing for this conference I had a dream about it. In the dream I was doing this Bible study with you, but I was not at the microphone. Instead, I was sitting in a back row, and I was going on and on in a way that I myself found boring, to the point that I wondered how it was that people were so polite and were managing to listen. Just then, a little kid got up, interrupted me blithely and said: "I have something to say!" He was maybe about five or six. Everybody was amused and relieved, including me. He went up to the front and didn't say anything, but he showed us the rough draft of this talk, where he had circled in red all the times I had written "God." He had also drawn a picture of a horse on the back of the page. We were somehow all energized by this. And then I woke up. I thought: What in the world did that mean? My three conclusions were, a little child shall lead them (that is to say, children can teach us something about hope), *God* needs to be underlined (hope is theocentric), and there is no real hope unless it includes all of creation (represented by the horse).

I felt a bit limited by this idea of leading a Bible study because that usually means doing a straight exegesis and exposition of a text, but what kept coming to me was more of a riff on the passage I had chosen, which is Galatians 5:5: "Through the Spirit, by faith, we await the hope of justice."

So I'm not sure if this is exactly a Bible study, though it is based on the Bible. (This is the kind of thing that happens when you ask a systematic theologian to do a Bible study).

The context of this passage is Paul's polemic against people who have opted for sticking to religious conventions rather than embracing the freedom that the gospel brings. Paul is trying to correct people who are in some measure pious, spiritual, or religious and are trying to live out the faith through some sort of concrete practice. In short, the people to whom Paul is giving a hard time are a lot like many of us here today. Last night Ric Hudgens spoke of this same kind of thing when he quoted that old 1979 Jim Wallis article in *Sojourners* called "Idols Closer to Home"—about the need to unmask our idols and to reclaim discipleship from ourselves.

The particular religious convention that Paul is railing about in Galatians 5 is circumcision. Paul does not say that the practice of male circumcision is in itself bad, but he tries to show that neither its presence nor its absence is central to the gospel of Jesus. Paul's point is that when we rely on religious conventions to give us freedom, we lose hope. Instead, it is for freedom that we have been set free by Christ. The minute we begin to make the observance of certain religiously endorsed customs and rules central, we start getting entangled.

In our case, of course, we are not arguing about circumcision, at least in this context. Rather, we are seeking to figure out how to reclaim discipleship in a postdemocratic society. But that doesn't mean we don't do exactly the same thing regarding other practices of faith that Paul's "foolish Galatians" did. When we get entangled in secondary questions, we risk losing the glorious freedom of the children of God, a freedom that allows us to live in a certain kind of hope.

If we are cynical about our relationship to church or to Christian communities or to the Christian faith, it is likely that our cynicism has grown out of these entanglements that fuse given practices carried out in a given manner to the Christian faith in ways that may be familiar and customary, but are not warranted by the gospel. To put it in Ric's terminology from last night, it may be that we are engaging in the kind of constructive cynicism that can serve as a weapon of the Spirit for the unmasking of idols. I would call this kind of thing a hermeneutic of suspicion and retrieval—it is the same idea. Paul recognizes this situation of entanglement and wants to clear out the tangles. (That's when he says, not very politely: If you are so committed to circumcision, why don't you just cut off the whole shebang? A case of hyperbole, of course.) Paul says that what counts is not legalism about exercising a certain practice of the faith, but "faith working through love."

Let me give an example of that dynamic that is very common in churches here in the States: flags and patriotism becoming entangled with the gospel. If we have a country or a geography with which we identify, there is nothing wrong with loving it, but when flag waving becomes a central part of a spirituality or practice that calls itself Christian, something is skewed and wrong, especially when the flag being waved is a symbol of an empire. If we identify with Jesus and are skeptical (or constructively cynical) of the use of his name or his message to justify flag waving, that is probably a good sign. We may become cynical in the passive, defeatist sense if we cannot seem to find any way to live out the faith of Jesus that is not entangled with the U.S. flag. But if we are attentive to the pull of God's Spirit, we will find that there are many spaces in which that particular entanglement is not central to Christian practice. At the same time, the Spirit nudges us to imagine possibilities for the redemption of all people and all of creation, including those who are entangled in these traps in ways we think we are not.

I doubt that many of us here are involved in the entanglement of gospel and flag. But we have our own entanglements that we don't see so clearly. That is one reason why community is so important. One day my family was sitting at the table, conversing over a meal. Our table in Evanston is at the exact intersection between a U.S. flag flying on the top of Albany House to the north and the tower of Saint Nick's to the west; so we eat at the crossroads between church and state. We were talking about the Bush administration. Our oldest daughter, who is in middle school, was thoroughly deconstructing W. and his friends in ways I thought were very accurate: she was criticizing the administration's bellicose policies and its indifference to environmental degradation. My husband and I were indulging in an enjoyable little moment of cynicism; I don't think it was of the constructive kind.

Suddenly another one of our daughters, who is a first-grader, burst out: "But it is not right to talk about Bush that way! He could change too!" She was reminding us of what we had taught her: that God is working in the world so that all people might be transformed and redeemed. She didn't like the way we made it sound like we thought this one powerful individual and his friends were beyond the reach of transformation and redemption. In fact, I was getting entangled in one of my own traps, that of embracing prophetic denunciation as a central practice of the gospel while too readily forgetting that grace and transformation are also part of the gospel. My daughter, who is also my sister in Christ and part of my community of faith, was helping me see my own entanglement.

So in Galatians Paul talks about "faith working through love." Sure, it sounds good, but what does it mean? And where does hope fit into that formulation? In answer to the entanglements that seem pretty typical of spiritual or religious types, Paul suggests a very concrete way of living out our faith, one that I think can bolster our hope and help us avoid the pitfalls that lead us to despair. He states: "Through the Spirit, by faith, we await the hope of justice." Through the Spirit, by the faith of Jesus in which we as a community walk, we eagerly await the hope of righteousness—or, as some translators have it, the hope of justice—that burns in the compassionate heart of the Father.

I find three important elements in this sentence, and the verse also reveals implicit and explicit Trinitarian dynamics in Paul's thought. Through the Spirit, by the faith of Jesus in which we as a community walk, we eagerly await the hope of justice that burns in the compassionate heart of the Father. The pattern here is Spirit-Son-Father, and it has to do with a movement characteristic of God's work with and in us: God comes to us and pulls us out of despair and on in hope toward what is to come.

Empowered through the Spirit

God's Spirit is the Spirit of life and of hope. Jesus speaks often in John's gospel of this Spirit, who as a Mother births us to new life, who is the Spirit of truth, who comes from God and is God, and who is our Counselor and Defender. Paul also speaks often of the Spirit, who intercedes for us, helps us, comforts us, liberates us, serves as the Midwife for our new life, fills us with gifts, makes us together into the church.

The Holy Spirit is the One in whom, by whom, and through whom we walk by faith. In the Greek text of our passage, there is no preposition to tell us exactly how to envision the Spirit's relation to us in the dynamic of being awakened to hope through the Spirit; the phrase can be translated *through* the Spirit, *in* the Spirit, or *by* the Spirit. God's Spirit is all around us and in us. In Romans 15:13, similarly, Paul speaks of how the God of hope fills us with an abundance of hope by the power of the Holy Spirit.

In his commentary on Galatians, Luther talks about how very feeble faith and hope are in the face of conflict and the cross: faith is but a tiny spark, scarcely felt. And yet the Spirit of God can whip it up into a mighty fire.[1]

It seems to me that one important way that the Spirit whips up the tiny embers of hope is simply by teaching us to be thankful. One characteristic of entitled, self-absorbed types is that they (or we) don't seem to be able to express or feel thankfulness in a profound way. In this, again, I learn from my kids. I've noticed that one of them, who just turned seven, has her own little liturgical pattern in her prayers. They always begin "Gracias Dios" (we talk to God and to each other in Spanish at our house). Then she thanks God for a number of concrete things (food, a place to live, a good time with a friend), and she earnestly reminds God about the needs of the poor ("Please, please help them find a comfortable bed to sleep, good food, a place for their things"), and then she ends the prayer with a final thank you: "Gracias Señor, Amén." Her twin sometimes says, "Why do you *always* have to mention the poor? God knows about this already!" But she persists both in asking for the good of the poor and in thanking God continually—in all things giving thanks. I think that her thankfulness is what allows her to nurture hope in God's provision for us and for the poor.

Being thankful connects us to the things that really matter (food, clothing, a safe place to be, people to love and who love us) and reminds us that everyone else needs those same things: give us this day our daily bread. The reason I think thankfulness is connected to the kind of hope that opens up doors and windows and lets air into our stuffy little dark rooms of despair, is that God is the source of our hope. Hope is all about God, as the little boy in my dream showed me by circling God in red ink again and again. Or as Jürgen Moltmann puts it: "The final ground of our hope is not at all what we want, desire and await, but rather in the fact that we are wanted, desired and awaited—by God."[2]

Moltmann is the theologian whose name will pop up if you put "theology" and "hope" into a search engine, and he was one of my teachers. I went to Germany to study with him because I had read his sermons and felt like here was a theology that you could preach and you could live, that was hopeful—not in the sense of the misplaced hope that Ric mentioned last night, but in the sense of a sustainable hope. It was not about optimism; it

---

1. Luther, *Commentary on Galatians*, 128.

2. Moltmann, "Meditation," 46.

was about seeing the world differently, with theological imagination, open to new possibilities that God may bring our way. Moltmann often points out that despair is a sin just as hubris is; medieval theologians and mystics knew this well. Why is despair a sin? Because our hope comes not from what we are able or unable to do, but from God.

If we wallow in despair, we miss out on seeing God's new and crazy ideas for life; if we are prideful and Promethean, we have no room for God's vision. Moltmann writes:

> The longer I have lived with this hope, the clearer it has become to me that our true hope in life does not come from the feelings of our youth, no matter how wonderful these may be. It also does not come from the objective possibilities of history, as unlimited as these may be. Our true hope in life is awakened and sustained and finally realized by the great divine mystery that is over us and in us and around us, closer to us than we can be to ourselves. . . . We are called to this hope, and this call often sounds like a command: a command to resist death and the powers of death, and a command to love life and to cherish it: each life, the life of all, all of life.[3]

Our hope relies on God, as manifested in Jesus, and the Spirit pushes, pulls, tugs at us to move us to walk in the way of Jesus. In walking along that way we will find hope.

By Faith We Walk in the Way of Jesus

The Spirit flings us out and forward into the way of Jesus. When Mark talks about Jesus going out to the wilderness to be tempted, the language he uses is that of being sent out there almost forcibly, expelled like a human cannonball. The Spirit is not always gentle, meek, and mild. Sometimes we are pulled out of what we were doing the way Ezekiel described it: yanked out of something by our hair and tossed in a new direction.

I had that sensation when I was trying to write this Bible study. I kept feeling that God wanted me to look elsewhere and do something else, but I didn't really know what. At one point I felt an impulse to leave the computer and go clean our rabbit's cage as a surprise for my daughter whose rabbit it is, and therefore whose task it normally is. To clean the cage is not as gross as you might imagine because the bunny is really very tidy and fastidious. I was conversing with him as I cleaned (in English and Spanish, as

3. Ibid., 45 (my translation).

he is a bilingual rabbit). The beautiful autumn sun was coming in through the windows, which were open to let in some nice, bracing air and also just in case the litter box was worse than I expected. The rabbit was quite happy about spending some time with one of his humans and also about the fresh Timothy hay I'd bought him that morning.

Unexpectedly I felt a stab of hope. I can only describe it as that sense of painful but also pleasurable tightening of the heart that sometimes occurs. I stopped talking to the rabbit and froze and asked myself: What is this? And then I realized: it is a sudden sense of hope, not the misplaced hope that we heard about last night, but that sense of going in the right direction. And why now, in the midst of the rabbit poop and the hay; why not before, when I was staring at the computer trying to think biblical thoughts about hope? Because doing concrete and material things, even very small ones, especially things that take us out of ourselves and our various obsessions, allow the Spirit to stir up hope in us.

The way of Jesus is a way of taking small and very concrete steps, one at a time; it is a way bound up with creation, with materiality, with actual earth and air and water and growing things. These small things are often our windows into hope, ways that connect us with the big structural transformations that are God's desire. We often make the mistake of thinking that religion or spirituality or faith in Jesus (or hope, for that matter), are disembodied, floating somewhere out there. But the way of Jesus was all about things like eating, and a healing touch, and walking toward Jerusalem one step at a time.

The disembodied idea of theology or faith permeates the ideological superstructure of many of our institutions. When I was a mom for the first time, and neither had my babysitting act together nor felt that it was right to leave my little baby for long periods, I took her to faculty meetings at the Baptist seminary in Buenos Aires where I was teaching at the time. As you know, tiny babies do just fine in meetings; it is toddlers who are too active to do well in that sort of setting. So I took her, and at the end of the meeting, since there were no changing tables in the faculty lounge, I put out a blanket and changed her on the floor. (I have a little theme going here, first about rabbit poop and now about baby poop. This is no coincidence, since I think that our hope has a lot to do with God's willingness to enter into our reality—not to use the more scatological term.) Anyway, as I changed the messy diaper, one of my colleagues said to me from a long way up (since he is a very tall man and I was down on my knees): "Oh, Nancy, to see you now! This is certainly a long way away from theology!" "Are you kidding me?" I said. "On the contrary, this is one of the most theological actions you will ever see. Remember the foot washing?"

I don't mean by this to justify the kind of unreflective pragmatism that is so dear to this society; nor do I mean to romanticize the backbreaking work of child rearing or cultivating the earth or any number of very concrete tasks upon which life depends. But when we walk by faith in the way of Jesus, awaiting intently the hope of justice, hope is born in our hearts through very concrete actions of the sort that Jesus himself both did and taught us to do. The Sermon on the Mount can give us hope because it gives us some very concrete steps to try out—but it also gives us hope because Jesus teaches us to be creative, imaginative, flexible: finding new ways to deal with our enemies, turning the world upside down, following him by the Spirit in the real, historical, material world. Jon Sobrino says that the point of discipleship (*seguimiento*: following Jesus) is to follow him in reality, not only in our intentions. When we do this (and it has to be a *we*, a community of followers in the past, present, and future, not an *I* only), we begin to discover an affinity with Jesus that allows us to know him.[4] It is then that our discourse about him really begins to be embodied, and with that embodiment of faith comes hope and the theological imagination to reclaim not only discipleship, but all of creation.

Our Hope of Justice

Paul says in our passage that we intently await the hope of justice. This expression is what grammarians call both a subjective and objective genitive: it is both about the hope characteristic of justice and about hoping for justice. The parable of the insistent widow comes to mind. Jesus depicts in a very graphic way her insistence, her stubbornness, her continued knocking at the door for justice. Her intense waiting for justice was not the waiting of quietism: she actually went and knocked, again and again, even though she knew the judge was unjust, corrupt. I don't know whether she believed in his possible redemption, like my little daughter might, but she knew how to wear him down. This is not the knowledge of privilege. It is the particular knowledge and insistence that poor and oppressed people have to survive, and it is a concrete form of hope. Jesus told us that if an

4. Sobrino, *Fuera de los pobres*, 157ff.

unjust judge listened to the widow, how much more will God, who loves us, listen to us.

I love the story of that widow, whom I imagine to be not very young, to be menopausal, at that age when many societies tend to value women less because their reproductive capacities are gone. This figure that Jesus gave to us as an embodiment of persistence in hope reminds me of a phrase of the Chilean poet Gabriela Mistral, who once wrote about *la porfía de la resurrección*: the stubbornness of resurrection, the pigheadedness of resurrection, the tenacity of resurrection, the doggedness of resurrection.

This stubbornness of resurrection is what waiting intently for the hope of justice is all about. We hope because Jesus was killed, crucified, executed by the powers—and yet he lives. The Spirit makes that resurrection real to us, not a fanciful story concocted by delusional followers, but the very stuff of eternal life itself. And that resurrection hope (as Moltmann points out) is *subversive* hope, it is a hope that leads to revolt against powers here and now. Real hope, as opposed to sappy platitudes or hard-nosed optimism or any other counterfeit version of hope that is floating around, leads us to live more deeply, in a more incarnate fashion, in a way that continues along Jesus' path of opposition to injustice. We intently await the hope of justice because we are aware of injustice and wait for the day when justice truly will roll down like the waters. The more oppressed we are, the more we understand the depth of that injustice. I think of our African American brothers and the way they are treated by the criminal-justice system; I think of the undocumented workers from Mexico who are mistreated by the same system that cannot function without them. But as things get more apocalyptic in this evil age, as we are hard pressed by the decline of this empire and its excesses, as all of creation groans, even those of us who are oblivious, privileged middle-class white folks start getting a clue about reality; and perhaps we too can discover that our hope, our only hope, is in the God revealed in Jesus. The way to avoid misplaced hope is to remember that it's not really about us, it's about God, but because God loves us, it is about us after all—and about all of creation—for God's sake.

We're Still Here

I want to finish by paraphrasing Paul in the words of June Jordan, the African American poet and activist. It is often poets and artists and dancers and musicians who show us how to express the hope of justice and the resistance to evil that is in Jesus' way. As a Black woman and a Black feminist, Jordan writes that she is doubly powerless: as a woman in relation to male power and as a person of color in relation to white privilege. At first glance, that might seem to be enough to lead her to depression or despair or full-blown cynicism. But she can see that simultaneously, and for the very same reasons, she is also doubly powerful, because women constitute the majority gender and "Black and Third World peoples constitute the majority of life on this planet."[5] From this paradoxical place she writes against the forces of death, especially the ones that oppress Black women; her words evoke in me an echo of the hope against hope of Romans 4:18:

> It is against such sorrow, and it is against such suicide, and it is against such deliberated strangulation of the possible lives of women, of my sisters, and of powerless peoples—men and children—everywhere, that I work and live, now, as a feminist trusting that I will learn to love myself well enough to love you (whoever you are), well enough so that you will love me well enough so that we will know exactly where is the love: that it is here, between us, and growing stronger and growing stronger.[6]

Jordan "calls the thing what it actually is," the way Luther says that a theologian of the cross should;[7] the way Ric challenged us to last night when he warned us about idolatry. She challenges us to resist evil. She knows she needs a community. And she trusts in the transformative power of love. God is the God of life and gives us life; God is the God of hope and gives us hope.

In a poem dated just after September 11, 2001, a few months before she died of breast cancer, when she knew she was dying, Jordan wrote:

> Some of Us Did Not Die
> We're Still Here
> I Guess It Was Our Destiny To Live
> So Let's get on with it![8]

Yes and amen. Let's get on with it.

5. Ibid., 270.

6. June Jordan, *Some of Us Did Not Die*, 272–74.

7. Lull, *Martin Luther's Basic Theological Writings*, 58.

8. June Jordan, *Some of Us Did Not Die*, 12–14.

The Philosopher, King

The Nature of Hope and Its Place in Nonviolent Resistance

by Gregory A. Clark

We commonly read Martin Luther King Jr. as an activist—as one who rallies the troops, attracts the media, and gives a good speech in the tradition of the black church. Yet King earned his PhD in philosophical theology. He studied the traditional philosophical and theological canon and carried on a constant dialogue with its figures and positions. Here I will read King the way one philosopher might read another. I will uncover the anatomy of hope and show where it fits among a constellation of concepts that shape the practice of nonviolent resistance. I do not claim that King's position was new, unique, or deeper than anyone else's position. Rather, I claim that his work was sustained by a clarity of thought on the nature of hope that gave substance to his nonviolent resistance.

Of course, King talked more of love than of hope. Hope is not the only or even the most important dimension of his position and work, but it was a present and necessary dimension. In King's most famous speech, "I Have a Dream," dream is the name of hope.

One of King's favorite statements, often given in slightly different forms, is: "The arc of the moral universe is long but it bends toward justice."[1] This statement will serve as a touchstone for our investigation, and

---

1. King, "Where Do We Go from Here?"

we will return to it repeatedly because it offers a helpful guide to the nature of hope in King's thought.

To say that the universe aims at justice is to say that all that is real is ultimately good. Hope has goodness in the form of justice as its object. Hope cannot aim at what is bad or evil. Hope aims at what seems good; we can hope only if it seems to us that the universe bends toward justice. Hope, then, is also bold. To many people the universe does not appear to be working toward justice; to them hope seems implausible, mere wishful thinking. Of this King was well aware.

For King, Friedrich Nietzsche was the definitive representative of the position that the universe is not working toward justice. According to Nietzsche, the universe is on the side of the strong, and the real world is the world of power politics that operates in a realm "beyond good and evil." All of us ultimately play by the rules of power politics, Nietzsche argued, even those who protest those rules in the name of morality, justice, or love. The universe is devoid of love, and professions of love are simply strategies of the weak to gain power over those with genuine strength. When I say, "I love you," what I mean is, "Don't use your power to hurt me." Further, I mean, "Let me inside your head. Because even though I can't control you physically, if I can get inside your head, I can get you to do what I want." We profess love in order to control people; everyone who has ever been part of a family knows how this works. But for Nietzsche, this was not just an interesting observation about family life. It was an insight into the nature of the universe.[2]

Let us grant that the universe can appear the way Nietzsche described, as a universe in which justice is only for the strong. (Gabriel Marcel wrote, "The opposite of hope is not fear, it is a state of dejection."[3]) King saw that this appearance is not self-sustaining. Rather it grows out of a nay-saying, a reaction against a certain presentation of Christian morality and Christian love. Christian theologians returned the compliment and reasserted Christianity as the denial of Nietzsche's denial. Both sides, however, agreed that an ethic of love and an ethic of power mutually exclude one another.

King differed:

> You see, what happened is that some of our philosophers got off base. And one of the great problems of history is that the concepts

2. See Nietzsche, *On the Genealogy of Morals*, Essay 1.

3. Marcel, *Mystery of Being*, 158.

of love and power have usually been contrasted as opposites—polar opposites—so that love is identified with a resignation of power, and power with a denial of love. It was this misinterpretation that caused Nietzsche, who was a philosopher of the will to power, to reject the Christian concept of love. It was this same misinterpretation which induced Christian theologians to reject the Nietzschean philosophy of the will to power in the name of the Christian idea of love.[4]

If Nietzsche's view of the universe does not allow for hope for justice for the oppressed, neither does a powerless Christian love, for "power without love is reckless and abusive," King said, "and love without power is sentimental and anemic." When "some of our philosophers" set love and power in opposition to each other, they misunderstood both.[5]

This analysis through dichotomies leads us to abandon "sentimental and anemic" love and to seek to attain for ourselves the very power we abhor in the hands of others. It makes us think that the only interesting question about power is who has it. This is the metaphysics of power and ressentiment with a vengeance. When Christians accept the dichotomy of love and power, Nietzsche laughs last.

This was not an arcane philosophical discussion for King. It has direct consequences for how we seek social transformation:

> Now, we've got to get this thing right. . . . What has happened is that we have had it wrong and confused in our own country, and this has led Negro Americans in the past to seek their goals through power devoid of love and conscience. This is leading a few extremists today to advocate for Negroes the same destructive and conscienceless power that they have justly abhorred in whites. It is precisely this collision of immoral power with powerless morality which constitutes the major crisis of our times.[6]

To the question, "What is the major crisis of our times?" how would you expect King to answer? I would expect him to say, "the race issue" or "race equality." These crises, however, find their roots in our inability to parse and answer other questions: What do love and power have to do with one another? Is this a universe of love and justice or a universe of power and Machiavellian politics? By posing the questions in a dichotomous manner, we short-circuit adequate answers.

4. King, "Where Do We Go from Here?"

5. Ibid.

6. Ibid.

King loved dichotomies too, and his rhetoric was capable of making them sing. But he knew that getting caught in dichotomies can have disastrous results. So King did not place a powerless love or a wishful hope in opposition to the reality of power. Neither could he place black power in opposition to white power as if that dichotomy captured the definitive question regarding power. He pointed us in a different direction. King's statement that "the universe tends toward justice" cuts through these false dichotomies. King joined the real with the good, the universe with justice, power with love:

> Power properly understood is nothing but the ability to achieve purpose. It is the strength required to bring about social, political, and economic change. . . . There is nothing wrong with power if power is used correctly. . . . Power at its best is love implementing the demands of justice, and justice at its best is power correcting everything that stands against love.[7]

King the philosopher defined power, love, and justice in terms of one another. The phrase "at its best" indicates that we can take this as a definition. A definition points out the ideal nature of its object, relating the properties that belong to it properly while distinguishing them from merely accidental properties or leaving out the accidental properties entirely.

When we plug King's definition into the sentence we are trying to explicate, the result is something like this: The arc of the universe is long, but it tends toward correcting everything that stands against love. This is a startling hope. It startles the Nietzscheans because it is the claim that someday the good will be real.

Even so, this claim can be interpreted wrongly. People can interpret King's hope as mere optimism. But optimism and King's hope are not the same thing; they part ways on the manner in which the future orients us toward the coming justice.

One could read King's claim that the universe is on the side of justice as a statement of optimism. In this view, humans and the universe are generally making progress. Things are getting better and better of their own accord, driven by an internal law that can be neither hurried nor impeded; all that is needed is more time. This is a version of optimism found among Southern moderates in King's day—and it was advocated by even Reinhold Niebuhr when it came to civil rights.

7. Ibid.

But this is far from what King meant when he asserted that the universe is on the side of justice. The universe does not move forward on its own, by some law of history, by an invisible hand behind the markets, or by any other automated process. In his "Letter from Birmingham Jail" he wrote, "How long have you been saying, 'Give it time?'"[8]

Whereas optimism positions us to wait passively for the future reality of justice, hope makes the one who hopes an active participant in the anticipated future. We hope to reshape reality neither in our own goodness nor in our own power. Rather, our hope draws strength from and participates in the work of God—or as King names it, in a "cosmic companionship." Hope is communal. To face the future through common work with one's companions, including our "cosmic Companion," differs from the resignation or exultation with which the optimist watches the gears of history grind on. The companionship of hope both requires and sustains what optimism does not: active perseverance: "Human progress is neither automatic nor inevitable. . . . Every step toward the goal of justice requires sacrifice, suffering, and struggle; the tireless exertions and passionate concern of dedicated individuals."[9]

The distinction between optimism and hope is part of the basis for King's distinction between pacifism and nonviolent resistance. Pacifists, King said, think humans are basically good and that their good nature will become more and more developed as time moves forward. That form of optimism underwrites passivity and offers the moral comfort of clean hands.

King turned a moral critique against the pacifist's moral comfort, arguing that pacifism tends toward self-righteousness and is indistinguishable from cowardice. King's criticism uncovers another, perhaps deeper basis for pacifism. The metaphysics of optimism—the claim that the universe and human nature get better and better naturally—do not suffice to generate the pacifists' passivity; nor do they provide adequate reason for King's charges of self-righteousness and cowardice.

Though King does not say as much in his writings, we might imagine the pacifist giving the following account of social action: In order to act, you must determine what to do, when to do it, how to do it, and why to do it. Once you have formed your best judgments and stepped out to act with

8. King, "Letter from Birmingham Jail."
9. King, "Case against Tokenism."

the best of intentions, your actions become public, even more so than your intentions. Events may unfold differently than you anticipated; things can go wrong. You may declare your intentions, but your actions will match up with those declarations only more or less. Others may and will offer alternative ways to read your actions. Their criticisms will have some truth, and you will have a share of responsibility, including the guilt, for the sins of your time. If you act, your hands may get dirty, even bloodied. If not your hands, then your head. So, action always goes beyond and sometimes even against one's intentions; inaction does not run that risk.

This account of action provides the sort of reasoning that King may have been criticizing. From King's perspective, inaction can reveal our intentions just as action can. Refusing to act so we can keep our hands clean reveals itself as self-righteousness insofar as it denies responsibility for the common life in which we all share. To the extent that insisting on my own righteousness prevents me from acting at all, my motive may equally well be described as a fear of action: cowardice. Neither pacifists' hearts nor their hands are clean; they have failed to show love in action.

King's alternative to optimistic pacifism was nonviolent resistance, or "realistic pacifism": a pacifism that is not "sinless but . . . the lesser evil in the circumstances." The pacifist, he said, "would have a greater appeal if he did not claim to be free from the moral dilemmas that the Christian nonpacifist confronts."[10] He insisted that realistic pacifism "is not a method for cowards; it does resist."[11] This was King's first principle of nonviolent resistance.

This does not mean that King simply reconciled himself to "breaking a few eggs," as do the advocates of Machiavellian politics on the left and the right. On the contrary, the word *justice* names not only the goal of action but also the methods of action.[12] Realistic pacifism requires not less, but more thought, planning, and preparation, for only in that way can moral principles integral to the goal of establishing a just community guide the action.

In the second through fifth of his principles of nonviolent resistance, King aimed to make it possible to move beyond a confrontation between the oppressor and the oppressed and toward a community where power

10. King, "My Pilgrimage to Nonviolence."

11. King, *Strive toward Freedom.*

12. King, *Trumpet of Conscience.*

corrects everything that stands against love. Those who resist nonviolently act with others on behalf of everyone: Nonviolent resistance

> does not seek to defeat or humiliate the opponent, but to win the opponent's friendship and understanding,

> is directed against forces of evil rather than against persons who happen to be doing the evil,

> is a willingness to accept suffering without retaliation, to accept blows from the opponent without striking back,

> and it avoids not only external physical violence but also internal violence of the spirit.[13]

Each of these principles deserves its own exposition to expose its grounding in hope. But because of limitations of time and priority, I will confine myself to the fourth principle: the willingness to accept suffering.

It is possible, perhaps even necessary, to consider King's position on suffering as part of a political strategy. He learned from Gandhi how to challenge a tyrannical government in situations where a Lockean dissolution of government or a revolution would be certain to fail. According to this perspective, King maintained only a pragmatic commitment to nonviolent resistance, a commitment he might well have abandoned if the strategy had failed to produce results.

While King never hesitated to argue that violence is impractical, this perspective about the strategic dimension of nonviolent resistance will not frame my approach to King's account of hope and suffering for three reasons.

First, King argued that violence was immoral, not merely impractical: "Violence is immoral because it thrives on hatred rather than love. It destroys community and makes brotherhood impossible. It leaves society in monologue rather than dialogue. Violence ends by defeating itself. It creates bitterness in the survivors and brutality in the destroyers."[14]

Second, the concept of strategy seems to imply that there might be other strategies by which one could reach the same goal. This position conflicts with King's explicit statements. Nonviolence is not a mere strategy, because as a matter of principle we cannot separate the means from the end: "Ends are not cut off from means, because the means represent the

13. King, *Stride toward Freedom.*
14. King, "Three Ways of Meeting Oppression."

ideal in the making, and the end in process. Ultimately, you can't reach good ends through evil means, because the means represent the seed and the end represents the tree."[15]

Third, in practice King's goals are of a piece with a nonviolent approach. To consider nonretaliatory suffering as a mere strategy is to overlook the substance of the things King hoped for. King's goal was not to win victory over the people who opposed him; it was to win them over. The friendship and understanding of the oppressor would not be possible if King's followers harassed, undermined, maimed and murdered the oppressor, as the oppressor had done to them. Consequently, the critics of King's nonviolent methods disagree not only with his strategies but also over the very shape of the future community. That future community was the object of King's hope in such a way that it defined hope's nature. For King to have abandoned nonviolence would have required that he conclude that hope is an illusion, that his dream was only a dream.

The close relation between hope and the willingness to suffer without retaliating becomes evident in King's many statements about suffering. We have time to consider only one, perhaps his earliest. Standing on his front porch in Montgomery after his home was bombed on January 30, 1956, King said,

> Now let's not become panicky. If you have weapons, take them home; if you do not have them, please do not seek to get them. We cannot solve this problem through retaliatory violence. We must meet violence with nonviolence. Remember the words of Jesus: "He who lives by the sword will perish by the sword." Remember that is what God said. We must love our white brothers, no matter what they do to us. We must make them know that we love them. Jesus still cries out in words that echo across the centuries: "Love your enemies; bless them that curse you; pray for them that despitefully use you." This is what we must live by. We must meet hate with love. Remember, if I am stopped, this movement will not stop, because God is with the movement. Go home with this glowing faith and this radiant assurance. Go home and sleep calm. Go home and don't worry. Be calm as I and my family are . . . and remember that if anything happens to me, there will be others to take my place.[16]

15. King, *Trumpet of Conscience.*

16. In Marsh, *Beloved Community.*

King offered various reasons for nonviolent resistance here. On the one hand, he appealed to the authority of Jesus and of God in a way not hedged by strategic concerns. On the other hand, he claimed that violence is self-defeating and that this nonviolent movement could not be stopped. These could be read as claims about which course of action would be most effective, but both reasons came together with the claim, "God is with the movement."

These claims do not make a case for a strategy of nonviolence; instead, they argue for the hope that when we act in concert with God, our lives will bear fruit. King repeated this early statement of his position—"God is with the movement"—in different terms when he commented on the principles of nonviolence, tying together hope and suffering. The hope that the universe is on the side of justice "allows us to suffer, because we know that we have positive companionship. Suffering is tied to this hope that the universe is moving in the direction of love."[17] This willingness to suffer has been noted by the best phenomenologies of hope. Marcel notes that "hope is akin to courage."[18]

I have devoted these few minutes to providing a hint of the fires of thought through which King's mind passed as he worked his way toward articulating his position of nonviolent resistance. It required all his mental and moral resources to refuse the dichotomies of love versus power, of clean hands versus broken eggs, of doing nothing versus doing violence, of white versus black, and of means versus ends.

King's metaphysics poses a challenge to those of us on the political left who have fallen in love with our self-justifying dichotomies. We love to speak truth to power. But of course there can be conflict only where two powers meet. Speaking is itself power, and power is not by its nature devoid of all truth. It is a false idea that some people (realists) have power on their side while others (idealists) have moral right on theirs. Those who seem to define power cannot actually define it. President Bush has power. But in Iraq, he has not been able to accomplish his purpose in the way he thought he could accomplish it. His power failed; Bush was powerless. Likewise, those who claim to define what is right do not themselves embody it. We all have power, and there are none so evil as to be without some right.

17. King, "My Pilgrimage to Nonviolence."

18. Marcel, *Mystery of Being*, 159.

King can help us see this because he had confidence in the educability of even the powerful oppressor. He saw a need to educate both the oppressor and the oppressed. The education of which King speaks is not a doctorate in philosophical theology. Even a good intellectual education, if it remains only intellectual, will produce cynicism when it confronts the workings of the various spheres of civil society. Although our dichotomies operate at the intellectual level, they are not only or primarily intellectual. We can neither fully understand them nor overcome them if we remain only at the intellectual level. King noted that he too required a supplement to his schooling:

> Living through the actual experience of the protest, nonviolence became more than a method to which I gave intellectual assent; it became a commitment to a way of life. Many issues I had not cleared up intellectually concerning nonviolence were now solved in the sphere of practical action.[19]

The text and classroom for educating the oppressor and the oppressed alike is the suffering produced by direct action.

Those of us who long for a different kind of power dynamic need to look closely at this commitment to nonretaliatory suffering grounded in hope as a way of life. "The arc of the moral universe is long but it bends toward justice." This is less a statement of optimism than a call to persevere, for the arc is long and there will be much suffering along the way. We need to raise longsuffering to an admired virtue and raise suffering well to a goal worth achieving. The philosopher King offers us this counsel as a life-giving alternative to our cynicism.

19. King, "My Pilgrimage to Nonviolence."

6

Cynicism as Therapy

Seeing the Log in Our Own Eye

by Dale Suderman

Today I am both a chastened pacifist and an equally chastened Vietnam veteran. But for this audience, my primary credential may be that my friend John Howard Yoder and I could often make each other laugh. I remember stumbling into the noted Mennonite theologian's class to take a final exam titled War, Peace, and Revolution—a year late. Several bright-eyed students, destined-for-doctorate types, challenged my right to sit for the test. Yoder growled, "Suderman has been in war, peace, and revolution longer than any of you." I sat for the test.

Much of the impetus for this assembly comes from a speech delivered in March of this year by Peter Dula, former Mennonite Central Committee director in Iraq. I have read that speech, and his despair and anguish are very moving as he recounts his experiences there.

The question before us today is what is to be done when the ideals of peace, justice, and truth are spoken and seemingly fall on deaf ears. The crisis of idealism is hardly new, nor is it insurmountable, but this is clearly a difficult time for individuals and movements. The problem, I believe, is not cynicism, but the need to reexamine our idealism.

Last night Ric Hudgens spoke about the ancient Cynics with some insight. I would simply add that being a cynic today is associated with being bitter and cold. But the original Cynics were a minor Greek philosophical school, often called "dog philosophers," whose thought stood parallel to the idealism of Plato. The Cynics mocked the pretenses of the emerging Athenian state, often violating public spaces—sometimes going naked and defecating and masturbating in public as a form a street theater calling for a return to more natural living.

When Alexander the Great came to see the wise Diogenes, a Cynic who was then living in a barrel in a public square, he asked if it was true that Diogenes had abandoned all desires. Diogenes replied that no, he did have one desire, and he requested: "Could you move a little over that way? You're standing in the light." This story may be apocryphal, but it remains illustrative: cynicism, whatever it is, is not nihilism, it is not bitterness, and it is not despair.

Plato and Aristotle rejected the cynical tradition and laid the foundation for our current Western idealism. The ideal both exists as a pure form in a heavenly sphere and can be fleshed out on earth. Plato's and Aristotle's concepts influenced Christian tradition—particularly the Johannine and Pauline concepts of Christ as the *logos,* broadly defined as the "truth" or the "word." In contemporary academic language, we continue this with the academic disciplines known as psycho*logy*, theo*logy*, socio*logy*, and anthropo*logy*. The major exceptions among the truth disciplines in academia are history and literature. There is no historology or literology.

The pattern of peace activists moving from being historians to being theologians—from the messy historical world to the world of pure types— would be worth examining. Both history and fiction have their origins in earthy and primal storytelling around campfires rather than in the world of pure types.

I know that there are other concepts of truth, and the noted philosopher Stephen Colbert has added a third dimension with the term "truthiness." But that is beyond the scope of this discussion. In the truth disciplines, the ideal is believed to exist—perhaps vaguely, but the ideal really is there—as first principle, best concept, highest good, best practice. And if it is discovered, it can be acted upon.

Now the idea that the ideal can be acted upon is not without controversy. Aristotle said that to merely know the good is to do it. The Apostle Paul admitted that he knew the good but was unable to do it.

For twenty years I have worked as a therapist, and as a therapist and as a human being, I deal daily with the problem of how individuals can know the good and do the good on an individual basis. Contemporary Western psychology and therapy continue to wrestle with this dilemma: Is there an authentic ideal and true self? How is it to be discovered? One can go deep within oneself to spelunk in the Freudian subconscious of the id, the ego, and the superego. Or be content with the Myers-Briggs test and the Jungian world of discovering our true inner archetypes. But unless this quest to discover our inner self is somehow connected to the outside world, it can easily become simple narcissism.

Two Jesus stories illustrate this problem. The first is Jesus' teaching that before critiquing another person, before removing the speck from the other's eye, we must first remove the log from our own eye. Jesus' image of imperfect vision, myopia, leading to distorted vision of both oneself and others is powerful. The second story is Jesus' dialogue with the Pharisees in which they contended that they would not kill the prophets as their fathers did. Jesus said that he would tell them a secret that had been hidden since the very foundation of the earth: You are precisely like your fathers.[1]

As a therapist I have spent years talking with alcoholics, drug addicts, criminals, and the mentally ill. That has been my exclusive caseload. A few of my clients meet all these criteria. As a rule, they are the most idealistic people I know. They can brilliantly spot hypocrisy, injustice, unfairness, and slights from others. It is impossible for me, in my role as a therapist, to live up to their high standards. But they can also justify their endless relapses and recidivism to criminal behaviors and chemical dependency because they see themselves as good persons who are doomed to live in an unfair world and who are entitled to find happiness in whatever way seems best for them. Their idealism is a core part of their problem.

One of my joking principles with clients is Rule Number 9: After age seventeen, you are not allowed to use the word *hypocrite* unless you are actually Jesus. (Children and adolescents either are in a state of sinlessness or lack the capacity to see the beam in their own eye. This is why they often require adult supervision.) Now a few of my clients do find the narrow path of humility and acceptance and do recover. Their struggle to do this reminds me so much of "normal" idealists—including peace activists.

It was perhaps the eighteenth-century Quakers who first used the phrase "Speak truth to power." But that strategy does not address the problem of what to do when power says, "I will not hear you. Now sit down

1. See Girard, *Things Hidden*.

and shut up." Marginalized people, be they criminals or Christian, peace-loving idealists, face the common problem of what to do when power will not listen.

The response of gangs and criminals is to affirm that institutional powers are so corrupt and incapable of justice that they are justified in telling lies to power. Another alternative is to speak "power to power." Mass collective movements such as labor movements, the suffragettes' struggle, the civil rights movement, and Vietnam protests have effectively mobilized power to create change. But their efficacy has depended on coalition building and compromise—strategies that often seem too cynical for pure-type idealists.

The purity of a witness against violence or injustice is often commensurate with its ineffectiveness in society. When we factor in additional principles such as our need for personal purity, our need to maintain our personal ideals in every situation, then a broad-based movement of speaking power to power seems impossible. The image that comes to mind is what happens when a vegan, antiracist, antisexist organizer seeks to build support against the Iraq war at a Teamsters barbecue. Which principle will be operative in that encounter?

Some Blanket Statements about Idealism

Whatever route we take when power refuses to listen, we usually have some explanation for the existence of injustice, war, racism, sexism, poverty, and environmental degradation—the opposites of peace and justice. But the alternatives are not often clearly articulated, and are even less so today because of the postmodern reluctance to make blanket statements about the human condition.

The problem with such blanket statements is that if they are true, then they are true also of us—because we ourselves are individually and collectively included in the human condition of original sin. This paradox is centuries old, and examples abound. As a rule of thumb, mainstream national identity operates on the principle of "Americans are good; the others are bad," while peace groups work on the principle of "Americans are bad; the others are misunderstood"—thus ensuring the peace activists' minority status in domestic society. But both thought systems deny original sin.

Despite the hazards of making blanket statements, I would like to make some blanket statements about idealism.

First, there is too much idealism in the world, and we are paying a terrible price for it. As the idealisms of Marxism and National Socialism have faded, they have been replaced by new demons of religious purity and orthodoxy—and even of "spreading democracy." The Middle East is now rife with overlapping and contradictory religious and political idealisms, and it is unclear how bringing more idealism will help a region already drowning in its own models of perfection. I recall John Howard Yoder offending both Muslims and Jews when he pointed out during an address at a conference that maintaining the ideal of the modern nation-state is in fundamental conflict with the peoplehood concept of space in the Middle East and therefore precludes the possibility of long-term peace in the region.

You see, idealism does not allow for compromise. If we are going to settle land claims and ancient grievances—some going back to the very dawn of history—we might learn a great deal about the history of injustice, but we are no closer to achieving peace.

Second, ideals are often highly fluid. This does not apply to anyone in this room, so you are off the hook here. But have you ever run into people who were evangelicals and then Marxists and then vegetarians and then vegans and then New Age and then into the simple life and then into radical pacifism and then got an inheritance and bought a condo? Each time they proselytize for their new ideal, but their intensity and commitment to the lifestyle of idealism may have—more than we realize—an economic foundation in our society of abundance. Philosopher René Girard points to a similar connection when he compares intellectual and political styles in France with seasonal shifts in the French fashion industry. We highly subsidized North American young and retired people have the wherewithal to bring peace to the exotic climes that we visit in our affinity-group travels —and to attend conferences where we give witness to our idealisms.

In Edwardian England at the turn of the last century a new term was coined: *liberal guilt.* The affluence made possible by the colonial empire allowed people a sufficient surplus of time and money to lament the growing corruption of British society. Good things came from this: settlement houses, reform movements, missionary movements, and attempts at socialist communities. But very few people noticed the paradox that their attempts at reform were based on the economic surplus in which they were swimming.[2]

2. Born, *Birth of Liberal Guilt*; Hartley, "Holiness Evangelical Urban Mission."

A libertarian historian recently observed that in our current age of abundance (as opposed to the mere affluence of the Eisenhower years) conservatives have learned to love the abundance resulting from a free-market system but hate the inevitable lifestyle diversity that it produces, while liberals love the diversity of lifestyles in modern society but hate the economic engine that produces them.[3] Cynical terms like *trustafarian* come to mind.

I know this fluidity of idealism is not consistently true and that these arguments apply to no one in this room, but I do claim the authority of old age, an ironic eye, and a historian's heart when I note certain changes in the idealisms of individuals over the past decades.

Third, frustrated idealism often becomes personally and collectively dangerous. When idealisms are frustrated, the fallback position is generally not cynicism. True cynicism is too ironic and detached for that. Rather, scapegoating takes over. We've got to find someone or something to blame for the failure of our ideals, whether or not that someone or something is actually the problem. Girard writes that in tribal communities the internal tensions of the community are assigned to a victim, who is killed in actuality or through a surrogate. Girard points out—and he writes as a devout Christian—that peace communities and other idealistic communities are no different from tribal communities in this. Witness the endless schisms, the debates, and even shunnings as we attempt to maintain purity by forcing out the heretic or the doubter, believing we would succeed if it were not for the doubters in our midst. This line of reasoning also produces the gulags of Marxism and the schisms in churches and families.

Scapegoating can also lead to conspiracy theories of bewildering complexity. Here the principle of *pharmacos* is operative. *Pharmacos* is a Greek word referring to an inordinately small object that is powerful enough to either kill or heal. It is the root of our word *pharmacy*: if you take a tiny pill it will make you well, or if you take another tiny pill it will kill you. So there is *pharmacos*—power in that very small substance. And so we have witchcraft trials where we blame the capitalists or the socialists or the homosexuals or the heretics. Blaming the Jews has been an equal-opportunity heresy because anti-Semitism crosses right and left divides, class lines, and economic boundaries. All of these groups can serve as *pharmacos* for us. It is their fault.

3. Brink, *Age of Abundance.*

When idealists are frustrated in achieving their goals, they too often ratchet up their idealisms into more complex, multilayered forms of personal purity, bitterness toward others, or greater zeal with even less insight.

Finally, idealism is often ahistorical. The subtitle of this conference is "Reclaiming Discipleship in a Postdemocratic Society." Stay with that phrase a minute: "a postdemocratic society." The assumption is that at some time in Western or American history we were once democratic! I am enough of an amateur historian to be curious when precisely this was. Maybe it was in Athens. I don't know! Historians are messy people. They note the complexity of change, often with irony and paradox, but they generally make poor activists. Don't annoy me by shouting out the names of two historians you marched with. Most historians just take notes and look on wryly and ironically.

For the most part, persons who have struggled for social change have contended that they were living in a predemocratic society. They were demanding that society and institutions live up to their potential for justice, equality, and fairness. If we are now working from the assumption that institutions are incapable of becoming fairer, more just, and more democratic, then we are living in a new historical epoch. But that assumption has got to be based on something more than just being frustrated because we are unable to achieve peace in the Middle East or some other goal that is important to us.

History is ironic. It is filled with unintended consequences. I remember speaking to a group of my fellow students at a Mennonite seminary in about 1972. I was speaking in support of the total withdrawal of U.S. forces from Vietnam, but I admitted that I suspected that this would mean great harm would come to specific South Vietnamese people with whom I had worked while I was in the military. My contention was that peace itself would not end the suffering. Fortunately, before I was peacefully lynched by a bunch of Mennonites for this heresy, a fellow panelist with decades of direct experience in tribal conflicts in Africa shared her experience of the death and suffering that can continue after peace settlements are achieved.

In 2006 I returned to Vietnam, where I visited the site of the My Lai massacre, my old billet in Ho Chi Minh City, and the imperial city of Hue. The massacres in both My Lai and Hue, one by American soldiers and one by the North Vietnamese army, are little remembered. In 2006 I saw a thriving country with a capitalist system that borrows more from Milton Friedman than Karl Marx.

My old mentor Delbert Wiens tells about an experience he had more than fifty years ago when he was the Mennonite Central Committee director in South Vietnam. When a street battle between warring militias broke out one afternoon, he and some Church World Service personnel heroically helped families cross a twenty-acre field to safety, with bullets whizzing overhead. At one point he took shelter behind some concrete blocks and realized he was hiding on the wrong side. In a telephone conversation just last week he told me, "Dale, I was too stubborn to admit that I was on the wrong side, so I just didn't move."

History, both immediate and long-term, is filled with such ironies and paradoxes. When madness is unleashed, there may be no simple solution. Peace in Iraq is what? More American troops? Fewer American troops? Partitioning of Iraq? All the options offer the risk of continued suffering. The madness has been unleashed.

Suffering is not new in human history, and neither is injustice. The church can witness against sin, but the task of the church is not to make history turn out as we would like. To believe that we can do that is to become part of the madness.

My friend Adam Schrag makes the observation that from a semiotics perspective even the term *nonviolence* is suspect because it leaves *violence* as the operative term. This brings to mind the image of a rowboat following a battleship. Despite the good intentions of the people in the rowboat, the battleship is still setting the itinerary.

Four Sources for My Personal Hope

My hope comes from different directions. First, the church is a source of hope. Today I am a convinced Episcopalian, even though I have a Mennonite ethnic heritage. I was long attracted to the church started by Henry VIII, which opposed the American Revolution, was once known as the Republican Party at prayer, and yet also provides sanctuary for racial, gender, and sexual minorities. Clearly such a faith community must have room for an ironic child like me. When I was confirmed along with other adults a decade ago, the bishop instructed us catechumens, "Do not add to the violence in word, thought, or deed." He did not tell us to stop the violence. He did not tell us to bring about world peace. He just said, "Don't make things worse."

A few blocks from here stands St. Luke's Episcopal Church. It is a lovely building. Walk over and see it sometime. It was built in post–World War I zeal, and it commemorates the war to end all wars. It has stones from the great European battlefields underneath the altar, and there are carved statues of World War I doughboys—American soldiers—lining the courtyard. The rector said to me, "There is no use trying to conceal this. First, this building reminds us of just how wrong we can be. And second, it also contains our yearning for a war to end all wars."

Tomorrow morning I will go to church and we will get on our knees and ask for forgiveness and admit that we have sinned in thought or deed because we are people who admit that sin exists both in us and around us. And we will affirm our hope as we do every Sunday: Christ has died, Christ has risen, Christ will come again. Though for the most part we are agnostic as to whether that is a pre-, post-, or amillennial event, this Christ-centered understanding of history is our hope. Our idealisms, ideologies, and social constructs are myopic: we see through a glass made darkly ironic and paradoxical by our inability to see our own eyeballs. We are certain that the church is eternal, but we are equally confident that it is made up of broken persons.

In a subtle way we will affirm the God of Abraham, Isaac, and Jacob, and the Father of our Lord. Platonic words like *truth, justice,* and *peace* are secondary to this prephilosophical understanding of history.

The communion rail is ironic and moving in most services. From generals to peace activists, gay men to homophobes, the economic elite of the city to the dispossessed of the city, we will all leave our pews and genuflect and walk down the aisle to accept bread and wine at a common table. In doing this, we recognize that we are participating in a larger cosmic drama going beyond our personal lives and beyond historical events.

And then the benediction will be recited by a deacon, with one portion of the stole going across the deacon's front then tied at the side to symbolize moving freely on the streets as a servant of Christ. "Send us now into the world in peace," we will say, "and grant us strength and courage to love and serve you with gladness and singleness of heart, through Christ our Lord." Notice that this does not say "to save the world." We are just to move through it as servants, deacons, and emissaries.

For nearly a decade this benediction has been posted just beyond my computer where my clients cannot see it, because posting it more visibly would violate the religious neutrality policy. But I look at it nearly every hour as I speak to people. The church is my hope.

Second, an apocalyptic worldview is a source of hope. A turning point for my worldview was when I saw a stage production of *Angels in America* in Chicago. As we drank coffee after that production, my friend John Kampen, a biblical scholar of some renown, shared his understanding of the apocalyptic language in texts such as Daniel and Revelation. "It was not the end of the world that preoccupied" the writers of these books, he said. "It was their vision for a new order breaking through that cannot be expressed in normal language. And so they were forced to resort to these wild images. Their vision is for a new order so radically different from the present that we are unable to describe it, and it goes beyond our hope for incremental progress and gradual improvement."

And thus I understood *Angels* playwright Tony Kushner's subtle mocking of political correctness, right- and left-wing politics, and religious orthodoxies in his stage play. His is an apocalyptic vision of angels in America breaking through for something radically new. Apocalyptic vision is a source of hope if we are able to see radical change that is not of our making. It is a source of hope for me.

Third, friendship is a source of hope. In his final teaching to his disciples, Jesus oddly instructs them to be friends. This stands in contrast to the alternatives. He could have said to be mothers or fathers or sons or daughters or brothers and sisters. Instead, Jesus chose this most humble, yet strangely intimate relationship of friendship as his final model for his disciples.

Friendships trump ideology. Friendships can trump the intellectual worlds of theology, politics, and peacemaking. Friendships can provide a sustaining sanctuary of storytelling, laughter, and tears—not merely about victories and accomplishments but also about doubts, failures, and pain.

I think we need to reexamine friendship because friendship is different from community and family. All three are valuable, but my own experience over the past decades has been that my friends—and they are a wildly diverse crew—are free to mock me, to critique me, to embrace my pretensions. And they are therefore a constant source of discipline and even discipleship for me. My daily hope is in friendships.

Finally, the scandal of the gospel is a source of hope. I want to end with a story about a man we should all know more about: the bourbon-drinking, straight-preaching Will Campbell from Mississippi. He is a good man, still living. Campbell was born in Mississippi, was a bright fellow, and went to Yale, where he was embraced as a white southerner who understood civil rights things. The National Council of Churches hired him as a civil rights worker.

One night Campbell was doing some late-night drinking with an agnostic small-town editor who shared his hope for racial justice.

"Campbell, sum up the gospel in one sentence," the editor taunted him.

"OK," Campbell said, "The gospel says we're all bastards and God loves us anyway."

Then the phone rang. A mutual friend of theirs, a civil rights worker and seminarian named Jonathan Daniels, had just been murdered. After they recovered from the shock, the editor said, "OK, so who does God love more, Jonathan Daniels or the racist sheriff who just blew his head off?"

"He loves them equally," Campbell responded through his tears. "That is the scandal."[4]

It was the beginning of a change for Campbell. He resigned his job with the National Council of Churches and went freelance, hanging out with Pentecostals and attending baptisms at the creek, working with black militants and folks outside the mainstream.

He was also willing to have prayer meetings in the homes of Ku Klux Klan families when their fathers were being sent to prison for racial violence. Campbell would say, "Their children and wives cry, just like the black folks do." He was able to move freely in all of these circles and he does to this day, defying categories. I think there is a powerful message in Campbell being so consumed by the gospel that he refuses to be part of any system or movement.

I know the scandal of the gospel can become an excuse for passivity or despair. But I think we can also see the scandal as a cause for hope, and therefore courage.

Our problem may not be cynicism so much as unfettered and unexamined idealisms, often the idealism of a naive worldview. The world will be saved by neither the idealisms of peacemaking nor the idealisms of the craft of war. As an interim ethic or at least a viable strategy, the options of pragmatism, social realism, and even compromise may be needed in areas of conflict. These do not necessarily contradict the deeper hopes that Christians have.

4. Campbell, *Brother to a Dragonfly.*

7

A Sign of Hope

Conversations with Iranian Religious Leaders

by Thomas Finger

One major reason for cynicism today is the increasing prevalence of violent conflict around the globe. While almost all nations oppose nuclear proliferation, several countries are acquiring weapons of mass destruction or are suspected of doing so. Meanwhile, various less-powerful countries and organizations are resorting to terrorist tactics that threaten to wreak destruction almost anywhere at almost any time without warning.

In response, the most powerful nations seek to crush all possible terrorist plots and impose economic sanctions on and threaten military action against countries suspected of developing nuclear weapons. Yet these superpowers fail to meaningfully reduce their own nuclear stockpiles, fueling cynicism about their professed peaceful intentions.

Shortly after 9/11 the United States threatened to attack Iraq for harboring terrorists and possessing weapons of mass destruction. The United Nations (UN) and many other organizations objected that little proof existed to substantiate either charge. Large rallies opposing the possible war sprang up around the world. Yet the United States went ahead. Half a decade later, many thousands of lives have been lost, billions of dollars have been spent, and no end is in sight.

It has long been clear that Iraq possessed no weapons of mass destruction, and that few if any terrorists were sheltered there. The U.S. government's own reports show that U.S. intelligence was highly flawed, and that it greatly exaggerated the Iraqi threat. A large majority of Americans now oppose the war, along with greater percentages worldwide. Among those who favor its continuance, many fear that a U.S. withdrawal would let loose even greater destruction. Countless people on both sides consider the megaforces that initiated and perpetuate this conflict far too massive to be controlled. All of these people are basically guided by cynicism.

Shortly after the Iraq war began, President Bush placed Iran among the "axis of evil," even though the Iranians had fought beside the United States against the Taliban in Afghanistan. Iran was enriching uranium, and the United States, with many other nations, feared that the uranium would be used for nuclear weapons, although Iran had no such weapons. The Iranians countered that the enrichment was solely for domestic purposes and insisted on their right to continue the program. But this was often expressed defiantly, especially by President Mahmoud Ahmadinejad, as if he was daring the nuclear powers to do something about it.

By 2006, the Bush administration was regularly portraying Iran as the main threat to world peace. Increasingly the U.S. government, which had and still has about 950 nuclear warheads on alert, threatened to attack Iran. The criticism and denunciation of Iran began to parallel the escalating demonization of Iraq before the invasion.

Although people and organizations everywhere urged the United States and Iran to enter constructive dialogue, both governments continued to hurl insults from afar, and tensions escalated. Once again it appeared that gigantic, uncontrollable forces of fear and desire for domination were sweeping events toward unavoidable destruction. Once more, cynicism seemed quite justified.

Nevertheless, despite these plausible reasons for cynicism, signs of hope were also emerging. Though the opposing governments were not talking, religious leaders in both countries were. I would like to sketch my unanticipated involvement in these conversations and draw from them some pointers toward hope amid the multiple pointers toward cynicism.

I should add that while I will challenge the Bush administration's international policies, I have no intention of being anti-American. I believe that these policies have greatly harmed the United States, and my aim is to suggest ways of reversing this damage.

The Conversations

In June 2006 I was invited, out of the blue, to speak at a conference on Mahdism in Tehran that September. The Mahdi is a savior figure whom many Muslims expect to appear at history's end to establish worldwide justice and peace. This expectation runs especially high among Shi'a Muslims, and Iran is the only Shi'a-governed nation. Unknown to most Christians is that Jesus is expected to accompany the Mahdi.

The organizers of this Islamic conference wanted to include a Christian perspective on Jesus' coming. They contacted Mennonite Central Committee (MCC), which contacted me and two American colleagues, David Shenk of Eastern Mennonite Missions and Gerald Shenk of Eastern Mennonite Seminary.

The keynote speaker at this conference was President Ahmadinejad. I was asked—very surprisingly—to speak first among the invited presenters (surely not because of any reputation I have as a scholar of Islam!). I shared my understanding of "The Coming of Jesus and God's Righteous Kingdom" with the large audience. Though many listened through Arabic or Farsi translation, I feel quite sure that these translations were accurate, since my address was printed in two different Iranian journals without alteration.

During this three-day conference, we Americans were interviewed frequently for television and radio. We didn't need to veil any of our views about Christianity or Iranian-American relations; rather, these were the main topics we were asked about. A year later, in 2007, I spoke at the next Mahdism conference and remained in Iran for ten days. I was continually discussing both Christianity and Iranian-American relations, in conversations and in many more interviews, some of which were filmed. Most of my interlocutors were in their twenties or thirties. They often prolonged these conversations beyond the projected time.

In May 2006, President Ahmadinejad had addressed an open letter to President Bush, who ignored it. David Shenk, Gerald Shenk, and I disagreed with some things Ahmadinejad said in the letter. Still, we felt that other points merited discussion. Ever since 1990, when the MCC helped in Iran's recovery from a devastating earthquake, surprisingly cordial relations had developed between MCC and some leading Shi'a theologians. Two international Shi'a-Mennonite dialogues had been held.

We three Americans met with some of these theologians, who are close to the government leaders, at Qom, the present capital of Shi'a Islam.

David asked several of them whether Ahmadinejad might appreciate discussing with American religious leaders some points in his letter. At the Mahdism conference, Ahmadinejad himself was quite accessible, and David asked him the same question. He replied that he was soon coming to New York for a UN meeting. Several days later his office asked MCC to arrange a meeting with American religious leaders.

About two weeks afterward around forty of us, nearly all Christians, met with the Iranian president in New York for about an hour and a half. We raised the tough questions: about nuclear enrichment, his opposition to Israel, his views on the Holocaust. This was the third time I had heard Ahmadinejad discuss these issues and outline his broader perspective in his own words. Some of his views disturbed us. But it was easy to tell, by comparison, that media reports of his remarks were usually distorted and taken out of context.

During this conversation, Ahmadinejad invited a delegation from our group to Iran. In February 2007, thirteen participants visited there for a week. They spoke with Ahmadinejad and former president Mohammad Khatami for two and a half hours. This was the first meeting of any kind between a current Iranian president and an American delegation to Iran since 1979. Perhaps it is not coincidental that several days later Condoleezza Rice announced the first formal meeting between representatives of the U.S. and Iranian governments.

Despite these cordial beginnings, opposition to such interchanges soon arose. Plans for the third Shi'a-Mennonite dialogue, to be held in Ontario in May 2007, were reported by *Maclean's* magazine and the Canadian broadcast system. These reports elicited some hostile responses but also some reasoned discussion. However, an expatriate Iranian group condemned the Shi'as' coming from Qom and vowed to shut down the meetings.

MCC invited this group of expatriates to express its concerns beforehand and to speak within the framework of the opening session. But after being admitted to the session, they shouted continually and managed to close the session down. Five of the seven expected Shi'a visitors had not even arrived yet because of visa problems. But after these five exhausted participants appeared, the remainder of the shortened dialogue, in which I was privileged to participate, went smoothly.

In September 2007, Ahmadinejad again visited the UN and was invited to speak at Columbia University. Columbia's president introduced him as "a petty and cruel dictator," and he was generally treated less respectfully than the year before. This time Ahmadinejad met with about 140 U.S. religious leaders. They again raised tough questions but received him courteously and stressed their desire for peaceful solutions.

Several weeks later, fifteen Iranian scholars were to participate in several dialogues in the Washington, D.C., area. These were to include two Iranian Christians and an Iranian Jew, which might have brought meaningful discussion of Israel into these kinds of conversations. But the U.S. State Department refused enough Iranian visa applications to prevent the delegation from coming.

Implications

The process I have described, of course, includes many more events and people. I have focused on my own involvement only to bring the story alive. Still, I have said enough to draw some implications for relationships between Christians and Muslims, between the United States and Iran, and, more broadly, between cynicism and hope.

Before I discuss these implications, let me emphasize something that virtually every Westerner experiences with Iranians: paradox. Neither politics nor religion nor anything else has just one face; whichever face first becomes visible is soon balanced, if not contradicted, by others. For example, Americans quickly notice the dress and other restrictions on women. Yet 65 percent of Iranian college graduates are female, and women hold many key business positions. Stereotypes of Iran such as those that pervade American media and political rhetoric are nearly always misleading.

Several tendencies characterize the current Iranian-American situation. I will phrase them in general terms to suggest that they may also exist elsewhere.

First, when government leaders are not communicating, religious leaders sometimes can. Even though the Christians participating in our dialogues were nearly all Americans, and the Muslims were nearly all Iranians, it was clear that these religions share some common ground. Foremost perhaps is the messianic hope for a world of justice and peace, which is Jewish as well.

To be sure, adherents of these faiths differ on how this future will arrive, and what it will involve. Iranian Shi'as expect that in this future Shari'a law will be imposed. Their Jesus, though he will come from heaven, will be no more than a prophet and will serve as the Mahdi's lieutenant. Nevertheless, the future world that both religions (and Judaism) envision will fulfill the true desires of all peoples for equality, harmony, and happiness.

Because they agree on certain features of this global future, these leaders can discuss how we should thus live in the present. They can ask what the shared values reflected in these features mean for current international relations. They can suggest and support approaches that are better than the current adversarial patterns.

Since the Iranian religious leaders are close to—and in some cases are—the political leaders in their country, such suggestions might carry some weight with the Iranian government. The American religious leaders' situation, however, is different. The Shi'a leaders apparently felt comfortable with the Christian groups involved in the dialogue because of their peace commitment. They sensed that these groups did not directly represent the American government, and they did not feel threatened by us.

It is of course possible that the Shi'as warmed up to us because they considered us naive and gullible. We cannot ignore this possibility. Although we are guided by hope, we must be aware of how our situation looks when it is cynically construed. It is true that naïve people cannot deal effectively with complex situations, so we must instead be, as Jesus put it, "wise as serpents and innocent as doves" (Matt 10:16).

At times, groups that maintain a critical distance from the corridors of political and economic power can open doors that are closed to power's representatives. This distance can make possible access to audiences that will listen to a vision shaped not by strategic realities but by expectations of God's coming, worldwide kingdom, even if it sounds strange at first.

Second, people want other people to understand their real views. Most Americans probably would not visit Iran, fearing that they would be despised, criticized, and even injured. But the Iranians I met, both at random and at scheduled events, were very eager to meet an American. They seemed almost desperate tell me how they really felt about Americans and many other issues. Iranians often asked why I had come when tensions between our countries were so high. I replied that these are the most important times to meet and try to understand each other. They always warmed to this response.

Most Iranians, like most people everywhere, find meeting foreigners interesting. They'd much rather be friends than fight. Let me share one of many examples. In September 2007, I had to travel alone by overnight bus from Shiraz (in southwest Iran) to Qom. Tourists hardly ever ride such buses. My ticket and every sign in the large bus station in Shiraz were in Farsi. Though I was clearly the only Westerner aboard, no one was impolite.

One passenger who spoke some English asked where I was headed, and I said Qom. At a middle-of-the-night rest stop, this man invited me to share a little food that he'd brought. At four in the morning, as we neared Qom, I asked him to read my ticket. He said it was for Tehran (two hours farther), but the bus could stop near Qom. "Will the driver know that I want to get off there?" I asked. "Yes," he replied, "because I emphasized that to him"—without my ever asking him to do so.

Stereotypes about Iran can obscure some paradoxical ways in which its people are open to us. Since mullahs in robes and turbans rule the country, we expect Iranians to be very religious. But about half the people are quite secular. They don't attend mosques and have few beliefs about anything. Many struggle with lack of purpose and an emptiness that they seek to fill with drugs, alcohol, and fleshly pleasures. Most Iranians know very little about Christianity. But many are interested in hearing about it, even though conversion is a crime.

Third, to promote war, countries demonize their enemies. I have come to doubt that any country will support the danger, destruction, and enormous cost of war unless most of its residents believe that citizens of the opposing country (or at least its leaders) are extremely evil, and that conversely their own country and its cause are extremely righteous.

When Ahmadinejad's UN visit in 2006 was telecast, his image was often placed next to that of Venezuela's Hugo Chávez, who had called George Bush "the devil" and had complained that the UN chamber smelled of sulfur. The announcers introduced Ahmadinejad as Chávez's "Iranian counterpart." But Ahmadinejad had never attacked Bush personally and had never used words like that.

Western media repeatedly claim that Ahmadinejad not only promotes nuclear weapons but wants to destroy Israel and denies the Holocaust. If this is really true, he can be equated with Hitler, and any measures that were justified against Nazi Germany can be justified against Iran. But how accurate are the last two claims?

Regarding Israel, Ahmadinejad has used a Farsi expression routinely but questionably translated as "wipe off the map." I have heard him explain his views five times, and it is clear to me that he means removing the name Israel from literal maps, just as the name USSR dropped off maps after the breakup of the Soviet Union. Ahmadinejad believes that everyone who has lived in Israel/Palestine since 1948 should vote for a government; that is, one state should be formed, and presumably it will not be named Israel. This is probably impossible, and any attempt to make it happen would arouse conflict. But it doesn't mean slaughtering all Israelis.

Also, I never heard Ahmadinejad deny the Holocaust, though I heard him discuss it often. He seems to assume that something awful happened to Jews during World War II. His aim is to challenge some conclusions that automatically result. What, he asks, did this event have to do with the Palestinians? Why was their land taken? If Europeans persecuted the Jews—for centuries—why wasn't land in Europe appropriated?

While Ahmadinejad's remarks are routinely distorted and exaggerated, they do raise legitimate worries. To my knowledge, neither he nor his government has refuted, unambiguously and consistently, the two crucial charges against him. Why not? He could raise his questions about the Holocaust's aftermath without being vague about its having occurred. As long as he and his government remain vague, as long as they do not openly acknowledge and condemn one of history's worst injustices, I doubt that they will ever gain credibility in the West.

Unless I am mistaken, Ahmadinejad allows these common impressions to persist because they reinforce his attempts to demonize Israel in other ways. This can win Arab support. Iranians are not Arabs, and while other Muslim governments are Sunni, only Iran's rulers are Shi'a. Most Middle Eastern countries, not unlike the West, fear an expansion of Iranian and Shi'a power. To gain their support, or at least to weaken their opposition, Ahmadinejad demonizes not only Western powers but also Israel.

Fourth, to promote war, countries prevent exposure to their enemies' people and their views. Demonic images of a nation and its rulers will be most effective if they appear in a void—against a backdrop of ignorance, empty of other information. My greatest surprise at the 2006 Mahdism conference came in actually hearing Ahmadinejad. He spoke more like a preacher than a head of state. In his hope for the Mahdi's coming and his exhortation to his listeners to prepare their hearts for it, I sensed a genuinely religious longing for holiness and justice.

This cannot, of course, sanction everything Ahmadinejad might do to hasten that coming. Many devout leaders have wreaked havoc in history. But the vision he expressed sensitized me to hear convictions and desires from some of my Muslim conversation partners that sounded much like mine as a Christian. It seemed increasingly possible that these might provide some common ground for better relations between our countries.

Why, then, do so many Americans suppose that Islam's future goals are simply conquest, domination, and subjugation of other religions? To be sure, the goals of some radical Muslim groups fit this description. But why do we seldom or never hear about Muslims' hopes for worldwide justice, peace, and harmony, much like the hopes of Jews and Christians?

Images of Iranian mobs chanting, "Death to America!" and threatening to blow the world to bits capture our attention. But from an Iranian standpoint, the world situation looks much different. Iranians find it very difficult to understand why they are viewed as the gravest threat to world peace. Three nearby countries—Israel, Pakistan, and India—possess nuclear weapons. Iran does not. Iran signed the Nuclear Non-Proliferation Treaty. Those three countries did not.

Even though Iran sometimes hides information from the Atomic Energy Commission (AEC), it often permits inspections. This is the main reason we know so much about Iran's nuclear enrichment, though our media seldom make this clear.

From Iran's perspective, disputes over uranium enrichment should be handled by the AEC. Most Americans suppose that the United Nations should also be involved. But who are the permanent members of the UN Security Council? The nuclear club. The United States deploys about 950 strategic nuclear weapons, Russia deploys about 750, France and China about 130 each, and the United Kingdom about 50. To Iranians, the UN hardly seems an unbiased forum for resolving such issues.

The Bush administration repeatedly threatens to attack Iran. American naval vessels, some with nuclear arms, cruise the Persian Gulf off Iran's coast. The U.S. military budget is nearly a hundred times larger than Iran's. The United States invaded Iran's next-door neighbor, Iraq, some five years ago and still has over a hundred thousand troops there. If you were living in a country with no nuclear weapons and had Iran's military budget, which country would you consider the greatest threat to you and to world peace?

As further evidence of Iran's violent intentions, the Bush administration repeatedly accuses it of providing weapons and fighters to America's enemies in Iraq and to Hamas in Lebanon. Such charges are very difficult to verify. But let us suppose that some are true. Then let us ask: How many weapons and soldiers does the United States have in Iraq? How much military support does the United States supply to Israel?

I do not mean to endorse whatever Iran does. I find it crucial to scrutinize its claims, as well as those of its enemies, through cynical lenses. Iran insists that it will not develop nuclear weapons. I would like to believe this. I hope they won't. But I can't be sure. I am no fan of Shi'a hit squads in Iraq or of Hamas in Lebanon. But if we can view things from an Iranian standpoint, something seems wildly out of proportion.

How can Americans so readily believe that a country with no nuclear weapons and only 1 percent of its military budget is the primary and demonic threat to world peace? One answer is that Americans hardly ever meet any Iranians, and hardly ever hear what they really think.

Finally, demonization and isolation are the opposite of true negotiation. The Bush administration seeks not only to demonize its major enemies, but also to isolate them. An understanding of Iran's history and its national awareness warn that this isolation strategy could backfire. Iranians believe that they have a unique heritage and a unique international destiny and mission: to prepare the way for the Mahdi.

Iran is proud of being a Shi'a nation in a sea of Sunnis; of being a Persian nation in a sea of Arabs; and of being heir to the Sassanian, Persian, and other mighty empires. Further, Iran borders not only on many different nations, but also on different major regions of the world: the former Soviet Union on the north, Arab lands on the south, central Asia on the east, and Iraq and Turkey on the west, with Syria, Lebanon, Palestine, and Israel nearby.

But like persons convinced of their own uniqueness, such a nation can lack long-term friends. A strong self-awareness can be accompanied by deep insecurity. Threats to such a nation can elicit fervent defiance, even paranoia. Isolation can push it to attempt drastic, desperate actions.

Strategies of isolation and demonization focus on what Jesus called "the speck in your neighbor's eye." To resolve important differences, we must first give serious attention to "the log in [our] own eye" (Matt 7:3). If we want to understand what others really mean to say, we must first scrutinize our own perceptions.

One good way to do this is to listen to our opponents, and to keep listening while we silence our immediate impressions and responses. As James said, we should "be quick to listen, slow to speak, slow to anger" (Jas 1:19). This is crucial with Iranians, whose remarks may strike us as highly paradoxical or even contradictory at first.

In the process of listening, we will learn how others view us. The very shape of problems between us may begin to change. However, we need not continue indefinitely to accept everything our partners say. After we are rigorously self-critical and "take the log out of [our] own eye," we "will see clearly to take the speck out of [our] neighbor's eye" (Matt 7:5). According to James, we can speak and even get angry—but only after sustained efforts at hearing.

True dialogue requires openness, patience, and charity, not passivity and naïveté. Genuine relationships require careful, respectful expressions of genuine differences. Skeptical or cynical interpretations of some things we hear can be appropriate—so long as we hold these interpretations very loosely as tentative hypotheses unless further confirmation appears.

I have not said that hope is incompatible with an awareness of realities that seem to justify cynicism. On the contrary, if hope is not informed by such an awareness, it can be escapist fantasy. However, someone might notice that while I have acknowledged that many features of life today seem to support cynicism, I have provided few reasons for hope. Have I shown that hope is a realistic option? Of what value, one might ask, are a few conversations among a few religious leaders when megaforces sustained by billions of dollars, mountains of weapons, and centuries of misunderstanding separate their countries?

Such a question often involves an unspoken assumption: that if conflicts among nations are to be overcome, the only realistic means are military, economic, or political. But is it always obvious that military attacks and political maneuvers do a better job than dialogue and other peaceful processes? Do wars and strong economic and political measures always work? How much, for example, has the Iraq war resolved?

Twenty years ago, few people imagined that the Soviet world's highly militarized police states could be toppled by anything short of conquest from without or violent uprisings from within. Soon, however, most of these governments fell with hardly a shot being fired. This happened when the voices and desires of insignificant, ordinary people—millions of them—united and refused to be controlled by the seemingly invincible ruling powers. Diverse groups within these countries put aside their stereotypes and differences to work together for what they all wanted.

Quite often over the last century, the wide-ranging, nonviolent momentum of masses of people who are outside their countries' political, economic, and military structures has initiated transformation of those structures: in El Salvador during the 1980s, for example, and in Iran itself, most notably in 1905 and 1979.

I don't mean to sentimentalize some abstract notion of "the people." I intend only to question the assumption that conflicts within and between countries can be resolved through military and political channels alone. When people who are outside traditional structures but deeply affected by them begin to relate transparently, they discover that they have much in common, even if they are very different otherwise. This kind of discovery is occurring in the conversations I have described. These conversations arouse hope in those who participate.

When commonality involves something as powerful as religion, especially a religion imbued with messianic hope, it can motivate people to think creatively about their situation. It can provide new reasons for hope that go beyond the conflicts they experience and the cynicism that these conflicts seem to validate.

At first, to be sure, these reasons for hope may seem weak and uncertain. Living by hope may not always bring the results we want; it provides no magic recipe. But some reasons for hope do exist in today's cynical world. Perhaps it is more satisfying, and even realistic, to heed those signs than to succumb to the faceless megaforces that we may think control us.

8

Sink into Cynicism or Soar into Hope?

Demonstrating Hope and Patience at Koinonia Farm

by Bren Dubay

"They who have an unsatisfied appetite for the right are God's people, for they will be given plenty to chew on."[1] I like Clarence Jordan's translation of the fourth Beatitude in the Sermon on the Mount. I'm particularly fond of the word *chew* in this context. It suggests that God's people will always be chewing, or physically seeking the right. And we have a lot to chew on at Koinonia Farm. We are constantly chewing on hope. We ask God to renew our hope, to allow us to demonstrate an active life full of hope and patience.

I often wonder why Americans travel about so much, why we are so restless. What are we looking for? Hope perhaps? Do impatience and cynicism go hand in hand? Though some people are called to be pilgrims, traveling from place to place, it seems to me that most people move about because they are chasing after hope and they are certain that it exists "out there." But is there value in staying in place and living through the good and the bad, the ups and the downs?

Koinonia's presence demonstrates that there is value in staying put. It demonstrates that hope resides within us, within humanity—within us as

1. Jordan, *Cotton Patch Gospel*, 8.

individuals and certainly within us as community. Out of this reservoir of hope comes action. Koinonia still exists today because a few people—and it has always been just a few people—stayed put and paid attention. This has required us to intentionally and consciously work on patience.

The Founding of Koinonia

Inspired by the description of the early church in the book of Acts, Clarence and Florence Jordan and Martin and Mabel England founded Koinonia in 1942 in Americus, Georgia, as an experiment in Christian living. We continue that experiment today. There have been many moments in our sixty-five years to affirm the scowl of the most hardened cynic, and just as many to justify limitless hope.

At an early age, Clarence faced the choice between cynicism and hope. He was a good southern boy in the small town of Talbotton, Georgia, born in 1912 and one of ten children. His father, a successful businessman, had started the town's only bank and owned its only general store. Clarence was a member of the privileged class.

As was often the case in those times, church was central to this strong southern family. And Clarence noticed at an early age what too many of us often notice within the church—that what is taught is not what is lived. He recalled that in Sunday school he sang, "Jesus loves the little children, all the children of the world. Red and yellow, black and white, they are precious in his sight. Jesus loves the little children of the world." The lyrics sounded like Jesus. But the red, yellow, black, and even some of the white children didn't seem precious in anyone else's sight. It did not escape his young eyes that the black children were not precious to hardly anyone he knew.

The Jordans' backyard adjoined the backyard of the county jail. As a preteen Clarence took to cutting through the jail yard on his way home from school, and he made friends with some of the prisoners. The cook took a particular liking to him and gave him fatback and cornbread every afternoon. Food—the way to capture the heart of a growing boy. Clarence conversed with men who were chained together at the ankles, and it did not escape his notice that most of them were African American.

Then came the revival meeting. On one hot, humid night when he was twelve years old, Clarence answered the call and joined the church. The choir sang and sang. One voice stood out above all the rest. The warden of the jail sang in a rich, deep bass "Love Lifted Me." At this revival when Clarence joined the church, the song on everyone's lips and filling everyone's heart was "Love Lifted Me."

That night he went home happy. Jesus had called him and he had answered yes. But his reverie was broken by sudden screams coming from behind his house, from the jail yard. Clarence knew what was happening. The jailers were using a device he had seen before. It was called a stretcher. A prisoner's feet were tied down, and his arms were tied up over his head. Somebody would pull a rope stretching the arms until they were sometimes pulled out of the shoulder sockets. A prisoner was being stretched that very night, and Clarence recognized the screams. He knew the prisoner by name; he had talked with him many times. And Clarence knew the man pulling the rope. It was the warden who only hours before had been singing "Love Lifted Me."

Likely we have all felt the way Clarence felt that night. There are so many reasons simply to walk away from Christianity if we pay attention to what many people in the faith are doing. The same can be said for Islam, Judaism, or any religion. At twelve years old, Clarence had a choice between cynicism and hope. He was mad at God. But as he railed at God that night, a thought came to him, "This is what man is doing to man. This isn't what God is doing."

So Clarence landed squarely on the side of hope. As he grew, he zeroed in on farming as a way to help his neighbors. He was familiar with how sharecropping and tenant farming worked. He understood that these systems held both poor blacks and poor whites in bondage. Putting his hope in agriculture, he went off to the University of Georgia to earn his undergraduate degree. But he wasn't to begin farming immediately. Something within him stirred, and he traded the plow for the pulpit—at least for the time being. God had called him again, this time to the ministry.

While attending seminary in Louisville, Kentucky, Clarence "fell in love with the Greek," as his wife, Florence, often declared. One word in particular caught his attention: *koinonia*. It means "community, holding all things in common, fellowship, commune." The koinonia is what the first small band of believers called themselves.

Though he went on to earn a PhD in New Testament Greek, school wasn't all studies for Clarence. He spent time serving urban African-American communities. He was an activist working for a cause, but something haunted him and caused him to flirt with cynicism once more. He recorded this revelation in his journal:

> The thing that just bowled me over was the realization that whites had the very things that I wanted blacks to have, and the whites were living in such a hell. Why should I feel that blacks would be in any less a hell if they had these things? There had to be something extra somewhere. I was driven in a desperate search for spiritual resources.[2]

He came to believe that the spiritual resources he was looking for could be found in a koinonia—a group of people living together, working together, and sharing all things in common, demonstrating a life rooted in the gospel. Service would naturally flow from there.

So in 1942, the two young couples, full of hope, bought a broken-down farm in southwest Georgia. The koinonia was born. Brotherhood and sisterhood, nonviolence, and economic sharing were to be its fundamental guidelines. Farming was to sustain it. Clarence's degree in agriculture finally would be put to good use. The Jordans and the Englands had picked the poorest county in Georgia, and with the intention of being good neighbors they had placed themselves among the sharecroppers and tenant farmers.

It was good for them to learn right off the bat that their neighbors could help them as much as they could help their neighbors. Clarence had book knowledge about agriculture but lacked the practical skills. The story goes that each morning he and Martin would climb up on the roof of the farmhouse to see what their neighbors were doing in the fields. Then they would climb down and do the same thing. Out of this living of their hope and being a neighbor, things began to happen.

One day when Clarence was walking in the cornfields, he met a young woman who he learned had five small children. "Where do you get the milk to feed all these children?" he asked. There was a long silence, then the young mother answered, "Well, Mr. Clarence, when it's hard, we try harder."

Koinonia had cows. That very day, the farm started a cow lending library. Neighbors would check out a cow. When the cow went dry, they would bring it back and get another one. Without any fanfare, they had been provided a means to give their children milk to drink. It was a very practical action, springing from a reservoir of hope.

When the people at Koinonia Farm noticed that white children had transportation to school and back but black children had none, they simply cranked up one of the old vehicles and began driving children to and from

2. Lee, *Cotton Patch Evidence*, 11.

school. I'm happy to tell you that we had the opportunity a couple of years ago to offer this help to our neighbors again. The Sumter County School district found its buses so oversubscribed that they couldn't transport every child. Koinonia once more drove children to school.

The Koinonians were doing many things, and they were hopeful, but hope has a way of attracting cynicism. The country was almost a year into World War II when Koinonia was founded. Set on modeling themselves after the early church, the people of Koinonia espoused pacifism and nonviolence. They were well aware that for the first three hundred years of Christianity, Christians did not take up arms against anyone. It wasn't until the Roman emperor Constantine made Christianity the official state religion that this changed. There was some frowning from local folk about the pacifist stance, but they knew that Clarence, Martin, and some of the others at Koinonia were ministers, and ministers were exempt from military service. They overlooked the fact that Clarence had tried to have his exemption overturned so he could register as a conscientious objector. Maybe they looked the other way because Clarence was a popular preacher and speaker. He would say things that caused people to frown and squirm, but mostly they smiled and nodded. The real hostility was to come later.

The koinonia attempted to demonstrate a way of life that they believed reflected Jesus' teachings. From the beginning, black neighbors sat and ate at the same table with them. This was against the law in the Jim Crow South. From the beginning, people of any race could participate in the life of the community. Most of the people who joined were white, but there were some African Americans who came there for transitional housing. Whenever there was any money to hire people to work at the farm, Koinonia paid black and white workers equally. They were trying to live the way of Jesus, trying to walk it not just talk it, trying to carry it out in everyday life. If they sang "Love Lifted Me," they wanted to mean it.

The Civil Rights Years

In 1950, there were rumblings that led to the expulsion of some Koinonians from the Baptist church they attended. It wasn't until 1954, however, that the situation turned dangerous. That was the year the Supreme Court heard *Brown v. Board of Education* and ruled in favor of integration of the public schools. The violence against Koinonia began shortly thereafter.

Would it be cause for cynicism if you were doing your best to follow the teachings of Jesus, and your neighbors began shooting at you, dynamiting your business, or cutting down your trees? In the mid 1950s, drive-by shootings became the nightly routine at Koinonia. But the people of Koinonia did not return violence for violence. Instead, they put up streetlights and stood guard, armed only with flashlights. They believed that their presence in the light might deter people from coming and shooting. It was a miracle no one was killed. It was a terrifying time.

It wasn't the physical violence that ultimately brought Koinonia to its knees, but rather the economic boycott. No one in Sumter County or even in the surrounding counties would buy anything from or sell anything to Koinonia. The Koinonians had introduced the egg business to southwest Georgia. Now no one would buy those eggs, and they were forced to slaughter thousands of chickens. They couldn't farm anymore, since they couldn't get the supplies they needed to farm. There was good cause to sink into cynicism, but the Koinonians chose to begin a mail-order business instead. Clarence used good humor rather than cynicism to respond to the horrendous situation; he coined the advertising phrase that we still use today, "Help us ship the nuts out of Georgia."

Clarence invented a peanut harvester to help farmers in Sumter County. Before this, it took sixteen people to harvest peanuts. With his invention, the harvest could be done with three to four people. He didn't get a patent, but openly shared his knowledge with others. Sometimes in our cynicism today, when we wonder how we're going to pay the electric bill, we mumble under our breath at him about this. We could certainly use the income from that peanut harvester today just as they could have used it then. If he were here, Clarence would probably say what he said then: if we had all that money, we might start talking theology instead of doing the work that needs to be done.

When the violence began, some sixty men, women, and children were members of this experiment in Christian living. Some were still here when the worst of the violence began to subside in the late fifties, but due to the economic boycott there were only three families left by 1963—the Brownes, the Wittkampers, and the Jordans. The farm could not support three families, so at a community meeting it was decided the Browne family would leave. Twenty-one years into the experiment, where was the hope? Wouldn't it have been understandable if there had been no hope left?

Atlanta must have looked attractive at this point. Clarence actively sought to sell the farm and move there, but instead he stayed put and paid attention. Using southwest Georgian vernacular, he created the Cotton Patch version of the New Testament. He preached, gave lectures, and was invited to present workshops at various places around the country during this time.

Then, in 1963, along came Millard and Linda Fuller. They had become millionaires early in life. They were living the American dream and had it all—houses, cars, boats, cattle. But they had lost their relationship with each other in order to obtain it all. Linda had left Millard earlier that year, traveling to New York to begin planning for a divorce; he followed her, and after a long night of talking and praying together, they reconciled. As they wept in each other's arms on the steps of St. Patrick's Cathedral, they decided to give all their money away and devote themselves to whatever God might have in mind for them.

Not long after that, they took one of the first family vacations they had had in years. While passing through Georgia with their two small children, they remembered friends of theirs who lived at Koinonia Farm. They didn't know much about the farm and knew nothing about Clarence Jordan, but they journeyed there, planning to stay for only an hour. They stayed for a month, and during this time began a dialogue with Clarence and others at Koinonia. Five years and many conversations later, the Fund for Humanity and Partnership Housing were founded. The plan was to build homes for people in the area, charging no interest and making no profit. Koinonia built 192 houses, and out of this work Habitat for Humanity was born.

Before even the first of those 192 houses was completed, Clarence Jordan died of a heart attack at the age of fifty-seven. Terrorism and economic boycott had not killed Koinonia. Would the death of its leader kill it? Cynics would say yes. But hope prevailed once more. Drawn by the idea of living in community and by the service work of building homes for others, people once more began coming to the farm. Even after Habitat for Humanity was founded as an independent organization and moved into town, Koinonia continued living its central ministry of hospitality. People came, and incredible things happened—people were renewed, organizations were born. And always, always there was a handful of people staying put and paying attention. One in particular, Florence Jordan, stayed put and paid attention until her death in 1987.

The 1970s saw a return to farming and the start of cottage industries. The mail-order business flourished. All this activity along with the home building gave Koinonia the ability to offer employment to our neighbors. Times were good in the '70s and '80s, but then came the '90s and yet another shift that led Koinonia toward cynicism.

New Challenges

In 1993, for noble reasons, Koinonia shifted the experiment a bit. Throughout its history, Koinonia's neighbors had been mostly African American, but no African Americans had chosen to join fully as members of the koinonia, to give up all of their possessions and permanently take on this way of communal living as their own. Community members were white, and the employees were mostly African American. So in 1993 Koinonia adopted a nonprofit corporate structure, shifting the focus to being a service business rather than an intentional community from which service to others would flow. The hope was that if Koinonia could add additional employment and leadership opportunities, perhaps that would attract more of our African American brothers and sisters to become involved.

The shift to a nonprofit corporate structure didn't work. The unity that had existed disappeared as the spirit of partnership and cooperation gave way to a hierarchical structure of employer and employees. The board of directors hired a series of executive directors from outside the Koinonia community who were not successful in generating the sort of income necessary to support a staff. Financial crisis engulfed Koinonia.

Within a year of the change, nearly all of the Koinonians who had come to the farm to live communally—some of whom had lived there for fifteen, twenty, thirty years—were gone. By 1999, those few who had come after the change in structure and had remained learned that the farm was a million dollars in debt and that foreclosure was imminent. Any self-respecting cynic would have shut the place down. But hope won out again.

Once more, a handful of people stayed put and paid attention. We quadrupled our prayer times. Like that friend mentioned in the eleventh chapter of Luke—the one who goes to a neighbor at midnight asking for a loan of three loaves of bread—we persistently knocked on God's door. "What do you want next from Koinonia?" we asked. "How can we best serve in the twenty-first century? We are your servants, O Lord. What do we do with this unsatisfied appetite for the right?" We were hungry for the answer to these questions, and the answer that came to us was this: "Keep working, keep praying, and keep inviting others to join you. Be obedient and return to the original vision."

So we have. In 2005 we recommitted ourselves to communal living. And God has blessed us with more diversity in membership than perhaps at any time in our history.

Through our shared life, we seek to show that there is a more patient and hopeful way of living. But here too it's easy to become cynical. It's easy to become scared and to ask, "Why am I doing this? Who is going to look after me when I'm old?" We need faith to live communally. And we need to support one another.

Koinonia is still called by God to community and to service. Today we are involved in a number of projects that allow us to share our life with others. Perhaps our most important ministry is that of hospitality. For sixty-five years now, individuals, families, and groups of all faiths have come to Koinonia to engage more deeply in a life rooted in Jesus' teachings. By hosting workshops and seminars, we seek to educate on a variety of topics, ranging from nonviolence to sustainable agriculture, from Scripture study to nutrition and healthy living. Our Heart-to-Heart home-repair ministry allows us to partner with neighbors of limited financial means to help them keep their homes in good repair. In addition to providing activities for local youth, the Koinonia Community Outreach Center hosts a weekly gathering for local elders to share readings, music, physical exercise, and personal joys and concerns. Through our Peace Action Team, we actively work to bring peace to our city, our country, and our world.

Koinonia has come face to face multiple times with situations and circumstances that would make cynics out of the most idealistic of us: violence, boycott, abandonment. But again and again, Koinonia chose not to sink into cynicism, but rather to soar into hope. The soaring continues. Nearly seven decades after the Jordans and the Englands began this demonstration plot for the kingdom of God, our appetite is still unsatisfied. We will always have plenty to chew on down here in southwest Georgia as we continue to stay put and pay attention.

9

Democracy and Mammon in Christian Perspective

Foundations of a Nonreactive Politics

by D. Stephen Long

The logic of the circulation of money in our global economy, and the logic of freedom and rights in our contemporary democracy bear a striking resemblance that is more than coincidental. These two logics need and feed off each other. In fact, they are finally one. They produce a political unity that not only denies any account of a common good or truth but thrives on protest against them. For that reason, our present political unity finds its ground more in evil than in good. However, a nonprotesting Christian faith cannot be absorbed into this logic. If a nonprotesting Christian faith were taken seriously, it could have a salutary affect on our understanding of both economics and politics.

The Logic of Money

What is the logic of money? As any basic economics textbook suggests, money is a financial instrument. It is not something in itself; it is instrumental. That is to say, it is a pure sign, a sign that bears no intrinsic relation to anything that it signifies. It can stand for anything that can be traded or exchanged. This pure formality of money, this assumption of money as "raw power" (as Jack Weatherford puts it in his *History of Money*) has distinct advantages for us. I do not need to travel with hard currency in order to facilitate exchanges as would have been the case in the Middle Ages. I can also assume that the currency used where I am now will be the same as the currency used elsewhere in this country. I do not need to exchange currencies when flying from Chicago to Philadelphia. This makes it possible for us to gather and become a people. And with my credit card, I would not even need to exchange currencies when traveling from Chicago to nearly any other place in the world. Money, as a virtual blip, now bears a formal equivalence that allows me to exercise its power without any sense of locality.

This exercise of the power that money is takes the shape of credit, interest, insurance, and speculation. As Charles Wheelan notes, these are the four "simple" uses for financial instruments. First, these instruments raise capital by allowing us to borrow money; in so doing they make possible credit. We borrow money we do not have today in hope and anticipation of what we will have in the future. Second, money stores and protects excess capital and makes the use of it profitable. It does this by establishing a "rental rate" for capital, the rate of interest. Like credit, interest allows others to buy into the possible future that our capital, and theirs, might produce. Third, money functions as insurance against risk. The future we intend to buy may not materialize, but through insurance, money can protect us against the nonrealization of the anticipated future. Finally, money makes possible speculation through futures buying. It allows us to gamble on risk even as we insure against it.[1]

What these four simple uses of money bear in common is their orientation toward a possible future, a future we seek to produce through credit, or faith. For this reason, theologian Philip Goodchild suggests that any critique of capitalism cannot be solely a critique of specific practices. Because money buys and calculates a future, it is much more than what its particular practice is at any moment. Money is now virtuality, a virtuality that knows no limits and no imaginable telos, so analysis and critique now require an openness to questions of metaphysics, religion, and theology that the standard Marxist, praxis-based critique has never been able to entertain. Financial instruments trust in a future that might be—a future that is not yet but is only promised and accepted on faith. In buying credit, I am buying a future. I am making an eschatological gesture about which Goodchild makes an important and startling claim: "If credit may lead to

1. Wheelan, *Naked Economics.*

creation, then, in a reversal of ideology critique, what we are may be determined more fundamentally by what we believe than what we do."[2] Our use of money is a form of dogma, for dogma is nothing but the common confession that makes a people possible. In modern democratic societies, our dogma is the value anticipated in our credit. This is our act of faith.

Credit is a store of value that allows us to live today on the assumption of a future possibility that we seek to will into existence. Now, that future may or may not materialize—as the foolishness of subprime mortgages demonstrates. Yet it is this projected future, this eschatological hope in credit, that creates a people in today's democracies. It is a pure exercise of will, an act of power that gives value to the world by imagining a future that does not exist against the one that does. This binds us together in concrete, material ways. First, it requires that we act in such a way that we privilege the future against the present or the past. Second, it requires that we protest against the present and the past, always envisioning them primarily as evil forms of oppression from which we need liberation, as times of darkness that wait for light. Third, we have concrete tokens of this political unity with us in the form of the currency exchanges that make it possible. They constitute a dogmatic unity that binds us together as a people, but one predicated on avoiding the potential evil that threatens us from our past rather than on any common good or truth that could unite us. These dogmatic commitments make politics possible.

Modernity often assumed that we had moved beyond dogma, that doctrines externally imposed were somehow behind us. The Enlightenment freed us from self-incurred tutelage and commanded us: Think for yourself. To which we obediently and not very critically replied, "Okay." We are gradually recognizing the dogmas of the Enlightenment: Think for yourself. Doubt everything. Be unique. Affirm your individuality. Be relevant to the moment. Always be new and improved. And we recognize these for what they are: dogmas that require acts of faith. In this recognition, in this postmodern moment, we discover that the question is not whether there will be dogma, but which dogma we will obey. In what do we have faith? Dogma can no longer be dismissed as an authoritative imposition we must do without for the sake of freedom. Rather, dogma makes our freedom possible. The political question is whether this dogma can produce a true and good freedom. What kind of politics does it constitute? Is it worthy of our lives?

2. Goodchild, "Capital and Kingdom," 143.

The Logic of Politics

The question of politics is this: What do we have in common? What binds us together as a people? This is a difficult question to pose or answer within modern democratic societies because they are grounded less on a good or truth that the people have in common and more on avoiding evil. What binds us together in our modern democracy is what divides us. In fact, the purpose of modern democracy is to protect us from the imposition of any common good we do not choose for ourselves. It does this by holding inviolate the right of each of us to willfully assert our own individual values against any imposed common good or truth.

In late-modern Western democracies, therefore, our political bonds are not forged from shared conceptions of the good. Morality does not bind us into some kind of solidarity. This is not just a theoretical problem; it has practical consequences. Raise questions of abortion, fetal-tissue experimentation, sexuality, gender inequity, the current war and we quickly discover not only that there are great differences among us, but that we have difficulty knowing how to argue constructively to adjudicate those differences.

The common good no longer functions for us politically; nor does truth. We know of no true object that binds us together and produces common bonds of trust. Some of us might find truth in Christianity, others in Judaism, Islam, secularism, or science, but we neither have nor expect a single account of truth that we can all affirm.

A famous court case in my own hometown of Skokie, Illinois, manifests how we are unable to allow truth to be the basis for our politics. Skokie has many Holocaust survivors. Several decades ago the neo-Nazis sought the right to protest and march in Skokie, denying the Holocaust. We all find the neo-Nazis despicable, and their denial of Jewish suffering blatantly false. But in a democracy like ours, they must be given the right of free expression even in a place like Skokie. They have the right of protest even when what they say is neither good nor true. The argument for this, which is persuasive in a democratic society, and which we cannot seem to get beyond, is that if we curtail the speech of Nazis we will have to curtail the speech of civil rights marchers or other groups we affirm when they come to town. Because we cannot get beyond this argument, we cannot figure out how the good and the true can function politically for us. Instead, the good and the true are always subordinated to a formal freedom—a freedom to differ that is protected by a right.

Our political dilemma is easy to diagnose, but solutions are hard to recognize. Who knows how to move beyond the subordination of goodness and truth to the formal freedom to differ in diverse and pluralistic democratic societies such as ours? This subordination of the good and the true to freedom and right has become our fate. I doubt that we can move beyond it. There are, of course, worse possibilities. I prefer the fragmentation of liberal democracy to the unifying power of any forced fascism or communitarianism, but it is unclear to me whether liberalism really does allow for the differences it trumpets. This is what makes it dangerous. When the freedom to protest and differ becomes the basis for our common bonds, our bonds are fragile and prone to be held together solely by violence because this freedom knows power only as self-assertion. It cannot give a reasonable account of what is good.

What we share in common is that we do not share anything in common, which is why we always say things like, "I disagree strongly with your opinion and I think you are wrong, but I affirm your right to express your opinion." Or the even more inane comment, "Can't we agree to disagree?" which is normally a sign that utter foolishness reigns. What binds us together as a people? The question is always already answered for us. The decision has already been made. Political bonds are forged from a unifying commitment to an abstract, formal freedom: that each of us has to give value to what is based on our personal preferences. And this prevents us from substantively good and true political discernment. Our political bonds therefore function in the same way our money does.

Money is a pure freedom, a raw power to exchange and consume not linked to place or to substantive conceptions of the good or the true. Its purpose is fundamentally to be able to call into question everything that came before for the sake of the new and improved—which is always about to arrive but never quite gets here. This account of money is quintessentially modern, the modern era being that period of time that takes its name from the Latin *modo*, the "just now" that we must prepare for by finding everything we have known or done to this point to be obsolete and in need of reformation. Modernity, like money, is a protest against everything old for the sake of the new that is about to arrive but never quite gets here.

While money does function as the primary common object of faith that creates our social bonds, it does so by hiding its dogmatic status. The hiddenness of its dogmatic status tends to make money reactive. That is to say, because money cannot explicitly claim a truth or goodness from which it can positively work, it can only posit an evil against which it reacts. The economist Joseph Schumpeter recognized this and termed it "creative destruction." Inadvertently, Schumpeter makes a case that the truly lasting modern revolution was not the American, French, Marxist, or Smithian, but the revolution of the accountants. He writes:

> Capitalist practice turns the unit of money into a tool of rational cost-profit calculations of which the towering monument is double-entry bookkeeping. . . . Primarily a product of the evolution of economic rationality, the cost-profit calculus in turn reacts upon that rationality; by crystallizing and defining numerically, it powerfully propels the logic of enterprise. And thus defined and quantified for the economic sector, this type of logic or attitude or method then starts upon its conqueror's career subjugating—rationalizing—man's tools and philosophies, his medical practice, his picture of the cosmos, his outlook on life, everything in fact including his concepts of beauty and justice and his spiritual ambitions.[3]

This passage should haunt us. We see evidence every day that Schumpeter was more right than wrong. The accountants now use cost-profit calculations to define everything, including the search for truth in education, with its preoccupation with outcome assessment; in justice, with mandatory sentencing regulations; in spirituality, with the proliferation of "spiritualities" as boutique objects we choose to fit our lives; and in the church itself, with the church-growth movement and churches' vulgar competition for market share.

Nonetheless, we still have places where the cost-benefit ratio does not completely define our lives. These are the sites we must examine for a nonreactive, nonprotesting politics. Take the family for instance. Seldom does the logic of money define it completely. We sacrifice for our children and spouses in ways that violate cost-benefit logic. Likewise, the university is sometimes (though certainly not always) a place where we still pursue truth outside the logic of money. Tenure, when practiced well, is an example of this. Moreover, teachers and students give themselves to pursuits of beauty, goodness, and truth often without counting the cost. The church is also a site that is ruled by a different logic or logos. I have not yet heard a Catholic mass or a Protestant sermon in which the priest or minister

3. Schumpeter, *Capitalism, Socialism, and Democracy,* 123–24.

stopped after fifteen minutes and said, "Now for a brief message from our sponsor: Today's mass (or today's sermon) is brought to you by Jones Funeral Home." Perhaps the day might come when these institutions also fall prey to the logic of money, freedom, and rights. But I'm skeptical that that can thoroughly happen. The subjugating power of the logic of money can never prevail over all aspects of God's good creation, because creation is good. Mammon can never have it all; the conqueror's path of money is not inevitable.

It is not inevitable for two reasons. First, the logic of money is not grounded in some rigid natural law, but in faith—a faith in both the logic of money and the logic of the modern nation. Second, we know the history of this logic. The unifying power of credit shows that our common bonds are acts of faith and not rigid natural necessities. This gives us hope, for it reminds us that there is another way. We are not bound by some inexorable natural necessity that simply had to wait until it could instill itself once the "irrational" logic of the Middle Ages was defeated. The logic of money was planned. We see this in the history of the rise of political bonds. Michael Perelman traces it in his *The Invention of Capitalism* by reminding us of the very different stories of the emergence of capitalism told by two eighteenth-century economic theorists, Adam Smith and James Steuart.

Smith began his tale with a pin-making factory. He did not say where this factory came from, or how the workers arrived at it. We do not get stories of enclosures that forced people out of the forests and off the land and into the newly emerging industry. Instead, he assumed that the form of exchange found in the factory just occurred naturally. People realized that one person making a pin was inefficient, but if they divided up the labor and came together into a cooperative venture, their work would be more efficient, and happiness would increase. The move from their homes to the factory to make pins was natural, the expression of an inexorable law of human cooperation.

Steuart told a very different story. He recognized that the original accumulation of capital that was needed to rationalize economics did not develop naturally. It required planning, policy, and even coercion. It began with laws of enclosure that forced persons off their small farms and out of the fields where they had self-provisioned. But it required even more than this. Steuart wrote for leaders who sought to rationalize the economy. He told them how to create "free hands" who would have no other alternative but to labor for an employer. This could be done, he wrote, through "authority, industry or charity." The purpose was to make individuals free from earlier ways of living by forming in them new desires and wants. Steuart contended that trade and industry could have the same effect that slavery had in the past: in slavery times people were forced to work because they were slaves to others; now they could be forced to work because they were slaves to their own wants. For Steuart this was positive, a move forward. But its success required intentional activity by political and industrial leaders.[4]

This brings us to a question about the freedom we associate with our common political bonds. Do our political bonds make us free, or is our freedom predicated on laws of enclosure? What must be contained so we can have the kinds of political bonds we have today?

The philosopher Alain Badiou suggests that what must be contained is any common account of truth or goodness that could fund our lives. Our lives must instead be funded by rights that are grounded in evil, because the assumption is that we must first be victims who need protection from others before we can be political agents. Thus, for Badiou, the language that we so often use as a way forward in politics—terms like *diversity, the other,* and *inclusivity*—does little more than maintain the grounding of our contemporary politics in falsity and evil. We already know that we live in a world with people different from us. In modernity this diversity must always be viewed as a potential threat, and so it is emphasized. Then rights can be granted to protect us from diversity by protecting us for it.

As an alternative to this, Badiou seeks a politics grounded in the priority of goodness and truth, in which the modern political problem is not one of recognizing the other but one of "recognizing the same."[5] For this we need a strong account of truth and fidelity to an event that will not fit into the currently prevailing ethical ideology. Badiou recovers Plato for this purpose because Platonism offers a strong account of truth.

Of course, Badiou is a false friend to theology. For him the good bears no relation to God, as it must for people of faith. Nevertheless, he notes that the reason we do not have adequate accounts of goodness and truth is not that we lack proper metaphysical foundations, but that modern politics and ethics police against such accounts. Our "enclosures" rule them out in the name of the freedom to express our difference, a freedom that has the

4. Steuart, *Inquiry into the Principles.*

5. Badiou, *Ethics,* 25–27.

odd consequence of producing common and even homogeneous bonds in the name of diversity—bonds we now rarely recognize.

Our emphasis on difference results in a sameness that prevents the recognition of common truth. Thus, Badiou writes:

> Respect for difference, of course! But on condition that the different be parliamentary-democratic, pro free-market economies, in favor of freedom of opinion, feminism, the environment. . . . That is to say: I respect differences, but only, of course, in so far as that which differs also respects, just as I do, the said differences.[6]

Respect for difference is a modern dogma that easily lends itself to the subjugating power of money in our lives. Money stores our preferences, producing a formal value that allows us to express our uniqueness, all the while creating political bonds grounded primarily in the need to have this freedom of expression protected—and we protect this freedom by ensuring that common accounts of truth and goodness become enclosed, cordoned off where they will not be allowed public expression until they first are turned into assertions of private preference. All kinds of public expressions of faith are permissible within such political bonds, and protest by one against the other is encouraged. This constitutes no threat to the political order, for these expressions are understood along the same lines as some people's preference for Fords and others' for Toyotas: personal preferences cannot and must not be adjudicated on grounds of truth or goodness.

A Nonprotesting Christianity

When we forge our bonds on the basis of this abstract freedom of self-assertion, we are tempted to obey a dogma that is grounded not in God's goodness but in a threatening evil. Our politics emerges not out of a goodness or truth to be received, but out of an evil, real or imagined, that must be reacted against: our politics is grounded in incessant protest. This is why a nonprotesting form of Christianity is so important—a form a Christianity that can assert unapologetically that it prioritizes goodness over evil and truth over error, while always insisting on the voluntary character of its political way of life.

If we are to have political bonds that allow us to truly exercise freedom, we will need a better answer to the political question of what binds us

---

6. Ibid., 24.

together than the exercise of self-assertion. The archbishop of Canterbury, Rowan Williams, recognized this when he wrote,

> To the extent that popular liberal and pluralist thought assumes with blithe unawareness a basic model of meaningful action in terms of assertion, it assumes a final social unintelligibility, an ultimate inability to make sense of each other's actions (which involves understanding so as to query and reexpress)—and thus raises the specter of the purest fascism, an uncriticizable exercise of social power in the name of a supposed corporate assertion.[7]

If our political bonds are nothing but this right of difference and protest, nothing but abstract freedom and value in a supposed future we choose for ourselves, then they are grounded in the priority of evil. If we are to have a common political life that is grounded in the fear that evil will have its day, then we need that evil, whether real or imagined.

But we cannot build a politics simply by reacting against this evil without reproducing in our political life the logic of the subjugating power of money. What we need are political bonds grounded in a common truth and goodness that show a nonfascist way of living with each other. This would have to be a nonreactive politics. It is not something we create as a form of opposition, but something we voluntarily affirm without assuming that our will produces it. Its affirmation has to be at the same time a reception of something other than our own assertion.

This is why the vision of the catholic, or universal, church remains so important—not because it is an alternative politics, but because it is a true and good politics that does not need to react against other politics in order to have unity. It offers dogma as a matter of credit: it imagines a future we do not yet fully know. But it claims that that future meets us now in the present from its originating source in our past. Like modernity, it allows for the emergence of the new. But unlike modernity, it does not require incessant protest against the past and the present for the sake of what is new. Nor does it fear the arrival of the new. Like modernity and its logic of money, this catholic vision assumes the inevitability of dogmas. But unlike modernity, it thinks we must explicitly express those dogmas and freely decide whether to affirm them in order to constitute our political bonds. The dogmas must be clearly stated as an act of charity, but no one can be forced to affirm them and their attendant ways of living. Likewise, no

7. Williams, "Introduction," 2.

one's individual will gets to determine what the dogmas are. Space always remains for those outside this catholic unity, while the unity assumes a fidelity to the truth and the good received.

This truth requires an undying fidelity and love, and at the same time a generosity toward others. Therefore it must have a place for liberality: for liberalism as a virtue to be exercised, not as a procedure to be imposed. Generosity can exist precisely because this is not a reactive politics. Because of its confidence in what it believes as true, and its fidelity to that truth, this is a politics that need not fear those who reject it. Because this nonreactive politics refuses to subordinate itself to power, understood as willful self-assertion, it will best serve the tradition of democracy by pointing toward something other than the logic of money and its inextricable link to faith in the modern nation.

In his book *Faith in Nation: Exclusionary Origins of Nationalism*, Anthony Marx demonstrates that the rise of nationalism could not occur until catholic unity was subordinated to national identity. Faith in our credit and faith in nation go hand in hand. This is why the contemporary fascination with the nation-state by all parts of the church—on the right and on the left—is so dangerous. It abandons what makes the catholic church political in the first place.

The catholic church refuses to acquiesce to the political claim that national identity must subordinate all other political identities, including transnational religious identity. A holy indifference to national identity by people of faith is not indifference toward one's neighbors, but an indifference to the claims national identity imposes on us because it inevitably requires reactivity. However, the catholic vision of the church is not oppositional; it does not categorically reject the legitimate claims of family, neighborhood, city, civil society, or even nation-state, for that would give those institutions too much power over our lives.

If we base our Christianity on our protest against these social formations, as primarily a contrast society that resists them, then we will need them for our identity. Instead our witness should assume a holy indifference toward them—neither resistance nor passionate embrace. Because we receive fullness in Christ, mediated through his church, our fullness always remains independent of these other social formations: it exists without them. They may have a limited place in God's economy, but they can never be made salvific and therefore they cannot demand the same loyalty as Christ's church, which is salvific. The church's task is neither to rule nor to be a vassal nor to be a chaplain, but to witness to Christ as Truth by making him present in the world through worship and discipleship. To gather in the name of this Truth serves the common good, even the good of those who do not acknowledge it as true.

So what does all this mean? First and foremost it means that the primary task of the church is to worship Jesus as God, to bend the knee to him and make a common confession. This is the political practice that defines Christian witness. If we lose this, we neglect the fullness that makes our faith the kind of credit that does not operate out of lack or opposition, but that proceeds from a gift that is inexhaustible. Second, the church shares a common confession throughout space and time because its unity is found in Christ. The language of diversity, inclusion, and difference is the language of commerce, which always assumes an evil against which we react for our particular identities. The church offers a politics that is not grounded in evil because it unashamedly sets forth dogmatic truths that produce a common unity. This is not a unity that seeks global imposition; its truths must be entered into voluntarily. And what this unity makes possible is a nonreactive politics that will genuinely allow for the common good to be honored—a common good that cannot be logically subjugated to the unit of money.

The political task of the church, then, is not to determine which political party or which economic system rules, but first and foremost to strengthen the transnational bonds of truth and goodness and their application in everyday political and economic life.

10

Personal and Communal Hope in Flannery O'Connor and J. R. R. Tolkien

by Ralph C. Wood

The fact that our world lies in moral ruin is a datum that almost no thoughtful person disputes. More people were killed by violent means in the past century than in all previous centuries combined—roughly 180 million slaughtered, most of them by their own governments. Stalin, Hitler, Mao, Pol Pot, Kim Jong Il; Buchenwald, Auschwitz, the Gulag, Dresden, Hiroshima, Nagasaki, My Lai, Rwanda, Darfur—these are the names and these are the places that epitomize our culture of death. Our task as Christians, though, is not to lose heart, not to become cynical, but rather to live by the hope that St. Paul describes as hope against hope (Rom 4:18). This hope lies beyond all human possibility; it is the single "hope that does not disappoint us, because God's love has been poured into our hearts through the Holy Spirit" (Rom 5:5). These rousing words from the New Testament are appropriate to cite now because our times are not unlike Paul's times. Our foreparents in the faith lived amidst a collapsing civilization, and so do we.

The question is not only, What shall we do? but also, How shall we live? My contention is that we must live in hope that is both irreducibly personal and irreducibly communal.

At the risk of embarrassing her, I want to begin by paying tribute to a former student who embodies the virtue I am commending here: the hope that is both personal and communal. As her name indicates, Celina Varela is Latina. Her parents worked mightily to see that she received a good education. She did. In fact, she finished at the top of her class at Baylor University's Truett Seminary, where I had the honor of teaching her. With such a fine academic record, Celina was poised to pursue virtually any kind of ministry that God might lead her to, perhaps in some prestigious place where her upscale salary would be commensurate with her fancy title. Thus would she make her parents proud, as we like to say. And yet the same Christ who spoke to the rich young ruler also spoke to Celina. He led her to get rid of all the possessions that would not fit into her secondhand clunker and to strike out for the Chicago area, here to seek an intentionally Christian and communal life at Reba Place. Thus she has cast her lot with this mainly Mennonite body in offering ministry to the down and out of Evanston, Illinois.

Not the least remarkable of Celina's gifts is her parents. They have every right to be disappointed, to ask whether all of their sacrifices were in vain, even to accuse Celina of throwing their sacrifices back in their face. They have not done so, because the senior Varelas are real Christians. They understand that Celina is paying them the highest possible tribute. They raised her not to make a name for herself, but to be a servant of Christ, to do work that the world doesn't bother to reward and to have hope that the world cannot comprehend.

Personal Hope in Flannery O'Connor

It is said that G. K. Chesterton once warned, "Beware of the person who wants to change the world but is uninterested in changing himself." "The Bible tells us to love our neighbours, and also to love our enemies," he quipped, "probably because they are generally the same people."[1] Hear Chesterton yet again: "The worst tyrant is not the man who rules by fear; the worst tyrant is he who rules by love and plays on it as on a harp."[2] In similar fashion, a Dostoevskian character from *The Brothers Karamazov* named Madame Khokhlakov confesses that she has no trouble loving humankind, but as soon as she is confined to a room with another human

1. Chesterton, *Uses of Diversity*, 50.
2. Chesterton, *Robert Browning*, 74.

being, she wants to climb the walls. Love in dreams, she concludes, is easy. Love in flesh and act, by contrast, is exceedingly hard.

These thorny and witty sayings point to the difficulty inherent in all doing of good, especially in the doing of good to the poor and the marginalized, the homeless and the hungry. That the needy need to be fed and housed and cared for is palpably obvious. It's a good deal less palpable, however, that our feeding and housing and caring for them, even though it may do them great good, puts us in great danger—not only the danger of self-righteousness but also the danger of neglecting our own souls. Social righteousness can become a subtle substitute for personal righteousness. In seeking the good of strangers we are always in peril of ignoring the good of our neighbor, including the closest of all our neighbors—namely, ourselves and our families.

Flannery O'Connor is a fine case in point. She was so thoroughly steeped in the speech and manners of her native Georgia, she confessed, that even if she had lived in Japan and written about Japanese characters, they would have all sounded like Eugene Talmadge, the quintessential cracker politician. Yet O'Connor wanted to write about the South—especially its fierce backwoods adherents of folk Christianity—from a critical distance, not from close at hand. She wanted the intellectual and artistic stimulus of living among fellow writers and thinkers, and for a while she did so, first in New York and later in Connecticut. But she did not remain there long. In 1950 she was forced to return to her hometown of Milledgeville, Georgia, there to spend the rest of her short life until she died of disseminated lupus in 1964 at age thirty-nine.

O'Connor feared that this return home would be the end of her creative work. She would have to place herself under the care of her mother, and she would be subject to what Karl Marx called "the idiocy of rural life." The small-mindedness of small towns is indeed notorious. It has been said of them that while nothing much ever happens there, what you hear more than makes up for it.

O'Connor dreaded the prospect of being scrutinized by local gossips and kinfolk alike, none of whom comprehended the radical kind of Catholicism to which she sought to give fictional life. They all wanted her to "do pretty" and "write nice," when her aim was to shock and offend both complacent secularists and smug Christians. Thus her stories often center on characters who undergo horrendous suffering and death—a grandmother and her family shot by a serial killer, a farm lady gored by a bull, a child drowned by his own decision, a preacher blinded by his own hand—all as they encounter what she called the mercy that wounds before it can heal. The protagonists who do not end violently come to a searing self-recognition that leaves them bruised and battered for life.

O'Connor was exasperated that even her own mother failed to comprehend that such violence was not gratuitous but was necessary to her art. But it seems slowly to have dawned on the author that she was herself in a perilous plight—in greater danger than the small-spirited folks surrounding her. I think that her reading of *The Brothers Karamazov* may have been the chief turning point. It is a novel that concerns the huge difference between love in dreams and love in act.

The four Karamazov brothers all have cause for resenting, even despising, their father. Old Fyodor Karamazov is a despicable creature. He is completely self-absorbed, caring for nothing but money and sex, even forgetting which of his sons belongs to which mother. This libidinous old rake has wronged all four of his sons.

The epileptic Smerdyakov is the son whom Fyodor has fathered with "stinking Lizaveta," the village idiot, treating her as if she were a spittoon into which he could deposit his carnal lust. Ivan is the son whose intellectual doubts concerning the goodness of God are due in no small part to his father's monstrosity. He repeatedly asks why God should let such a man live. Dmitri has been cuckolded by his own father, who seduced the woman whom Dmitri hoped to marry, the prostitute Grushenka. Alyosha, the future monk, is utterly appalled at his father's buffoonish violation of everything holy, especially the monastery where Alyosha lives as a novice. In sum, all four sons are justified in scorning their father. One of them, Smerdyakov, finally murders Fyodor, his deed prompted by Ivan's nihilistic philosophy, which holds that "If God is dead, all things are permitted."

Yet Dostoevsky does not permit his readers to feel that justice has at last been done, that we can rejoice that the world is at last rid of a brute who deserved to die. On the contrary, the novel reveals that parricide is the deadliest of crimes; indeed, it is a substitute for deicide. The killing of parents—assigning them the neglect and despair of nursing homes is but one of our many nonviolent means for doing so—is tantamount to the slaying of God. Dostoevsky's basic claim is that we stand in ultimate relation to God as we stand in immediate relation to our parents, at least in one particular and fundamental way: however unjust they may be, however much harm they may inflict on us, they nonetheless remain the source of our being. We owe them an unpayable debt, the debt of our own existence. Our regard for them, therefore, is a sure indicator of our regard for God. Parricide equals deicide.

Flannery O'Connor came to recognize, I am convinced, that insofar as she scorned her mother and her immediate family and friends for their religious complacency and opacity, she was herself guilty of the deadliest sin, pride. The Latin word for it is *superbia*. Its root metaphor indicates that to be proud is to hold oneself above and to look down on others, often with cold contempt. Flannery O'Connor came to see that while her devout Catholic faith gave her an acute spiritual discernment of the sins of others, especially unbelievers, it threatened to blind her to an even worse evil. She was tempted to a parricidal scorn for the immediate sources of her life—her mother, her relations, her Georgia hometown.

In Dostoevskian terms, she was drawn to love God in dreams when her insistent need was to love God in act, especially in love of neighbor. The word *neighbor* literally means "the nigh one," the one close at hand, the one next-door, the one in the same house, in the same room—even and especially the parent. Here at Reba Place, you are perhaps far removed from the familial and geographical sources of your life, from the people and places that made you. But you are not to forget them, much less to neglect them while you are caring for others far away from home. They are the original source of your identity, the rock from which you were hewn.

The upshot in Flannery O'Connor's case is that her fiction took a radical turn. Her novels and stories were still populated with smothering mothers and annoying cousins and self-congratulating secularists, but these were not the real miscreants. Instead, the miscreants were the thankless sons and daughters who lived off the largesse of their often small-minded parents while holding them in great disdain for not embracing "advanced" views on race and religion. This is especially true of two stories, "Everything That Rises Must Converge" and "The Enduring Chill." They both feature social reformers, they both are concerned with race relations, and they both depict sons who are enlightened about such matters to the same degree that their mothers are benighted. Yet in both stories the socially righteous protagonists turn out to be guilty of far worse evils than their retrograde parents. As alleged racial liberators, they prove more bigoted than their racist parents.

In "Everything That Rises Must Converge," the protagonist is a failed writer named Julian, who lives at home with his unnamed widowed mother.

Since the story is narrated from Julian's point of view, the mother's anonymity indicates how little he cares for her. Julian decides to demonstrate his own liberation from conventional racial mores by deliberately taking a seat next to a black man on a recently desegregated bus. The man immediately penetrates the pretense of his new "friend," seeing that Julian wants to use him as a tool for practicing his own moral hygiene. The black man will have none of it. Yet Julian is so obsessed with casting the racist mote out of his mother's eye that he remains blind to the beamlike presumption and ingratitude that afflict his own vision. Julian can "love" the anonymous Negro whom he does not know, but not the mother whom he does know and who also knows him (see 1 John 4:20).

Though conventionally prejudiced, Julian's mother is capable of the love that matters most: she cares deeply about her own uncaring son. And though she employs the usual racial epithets, she is no vicious racist. On the contrary, she accepts the hard lesson in racial equality that she is forced to learn. Across the aisle Julian's mother discovers a black woman wearing a purple hat that is identical to the one that she herself recently purchased, sure at the time that only her higher class of people could afford it. Julian seizes on this moment of recognition to humiliate his mother and makes sure that she detects his delight in her humiliation. Meanwhile, Julian's friendly and outgoing mother, who could have been soured by the revelation that she is no longer "better" than prosperous Negroes, plays peekaboo with the little boy whose mother wears the matching hat, and the child in turn is drawn to the white lady's jovial affection. In her innocence of heart, Julian's mother gives the boy a shiny copper coin as she leaves the bus. The black child's mother is infuriated. Blinded by racial rage and unable to distinguish a kindly from a condescending gesture, the black woman strikes Julian's mother to the ground, causing her to suffer a fatal stroke.

Addled and dying, Julian's mother remains gracious rather than bitter. She calls out for Caroline, the black nanny who cared for her when she was a child, remembering the nurse who gave her the unqualified love that her own son has refused to grant. Instead of rushing to her aid, Julian lectures his dying mother for having failed to recognize that liberated blacks will no longer accept white handouts. Julian's mother dies not so much from the blow struck by the black woman as from the racial righteousness of her own son. In the name of an abstract sense of justice for people he does not really care about, Julian has denied the most fundamental of all loves: the love of a son for the mother who not only gave him birth but nourished his ne'er-do-well life.

The fundamental lesson about hope to be learned from Flannery O'Connor is that hope can never be anything less than personal. Hope must arise out of our individual engagement with the love of God, and we neglect the state of our own souls at the peril of becoming something even worse than unrighteous—namely, demons of righteousness. Julian had sought to give hope to others whom he knew only at a distance while neglecting to give to his closest neighbor of all: his own mother. Hence the need for those who engage in difficult ministry to be concerned about the primacy of personal faith and hope and humility, lest the doing of good for others lead to a sinful disregard for those who are sometimes the most uncomfortable neighbors, those who have given us our lives.

Communal Hope in the Works of J. R. R. Tolkien

If the necessity of personal hope is the prime reminder to be gleaned from Flannery O'Connor's fiction, the necessity of communal hope is what J. R. R. Tolkien can teach us. Our times are beyond ordinary hope. I have referred to ours as an Age of Ashes, so prominent have been its bonfires of human flesh—from Treblinka and Nagasaki to My Lai and the World Trade Center. Yet it is not political evil alone that makes ours a culture of death. As the title of this conference suggests, we may well be witnessing the collapse of democracy itself. Democratic freedom does not always and automatically issue in democratic wisdom. Our fallen species often votes for what we want rather than what we need. None of Hitler's acts were technically illegal, since he was elected by a plurality of voters and all of his heinous death-camp measures were promulgated by duly passed laws.

A similar collapse of democracy is happening in our own time. There is fearful truth in the vision of Dostoevsky's Grand Inquisitor, again from *The Brothers Karamazov*. In that horrific nightmare vision, an alleged representative of the church upbraids Jesus for having sought to give people liberty when what we really demand is security. So it is in our time. The left asks the state protect everyone, without regard to merit or incentive, from both economic and personal failure. The right demands that the state promote the acquisitive instinct, so that the wealthy few are able to cushion themselves with ever more comforts and conveniences while the poor are given the leftovers.

What then is to be done? How shall we live? What is our hope? Tolkien's fiction offers tough-minded answers. Tolkien experienced the collapse of modern civilization with the onslaught of World War I. He fought at the Battle of the Somme, perhaps the most useless case of bloodletting in history. Many of his war memories make their way into his work, especially his masterpiece *The Lord of the Rings*. Though it is a massive, triple-decker work of epic fantasy set long before the Christian era, Tolkien imbues it with profound instances of Christian hope in these three ways (among others): in friendship, in vision, and in endurance.

Tolkien has a deeply communal vision of life. He understands that the Christian faith is not an inward and private thing so much as an outward and public existence animated by the sacraments and practices of the church. As almost everyone knows from having seen the movies, the central battle is between opposing communities. A small band of nine walkers is commissioned to defeat the mightiest of earthly tyrants, Sauron and his nine riders, called the ringwraiths.

The seemingly impossible task of the Company of Nine is to keep Sauron, the ruthless maker and ruler of the One Ruling Ring, from reacquiring the Ring now that it has come into their possession. In a show of immense wisdom and courage, they decide not to use the all-commanding Ring against Sauron, lest in destroying evil with evil they become like him. Instead, they vow to destroy the Ring itself. It is obvious that they cannot accomplish such a mission by sheer might, since they are small in size and without great physical strength. Yet the company has one asset that Sauron, despite his many powers, utterly lacks: they are a company of friends who trust each other so deeply that nothing can break their bonds. Sauron, by contrast, has not a single friend. He has thousands of slaves who do his bidding because he has coerced their will into his employ, but he has no friend in whom he can confide without danger of betrayal. He is the strongest of lords but also the loneliest and thus also the weakest.

In his celebrated chapter on friendship in the *Nicomachean Ethics*, Aristotle declares that no person, given the choice, would live without friends. He also says that friends are those to whom one desires to give the best of all gifts. In *The Lord of the Rings*, that gift is loyalty and obedience to the highest and worthiest of causes: the destruction of the all-commanding Ring. And Tolkien demonstrates that friendship is also the greatest of gifts because it can be given by the weakest and lowliest even more than by the highest and mightiest.

This paradox is made evident when the company is being formed. The choices for the first seven places in the company seem obvious. There are two hobbits, Frodo the ringbearer and his dear friend and sidekick Samwise Gamgee, called Sam. There are two historic enemies, Legolas the elf and Gimli the dwarf, who eventually become lasting friends. There are two strong men, the brave warrior Boromir and the disguised King Aragorn, also known as Strider. And of course there is Gandalf the wizard, the immensely wise one who is their real leader and guide.

Filling the last two places is more difficult. Elrond the elflord assumes that creatures of his own kind must occupy them because the lordly elves are both strong and brilliant. Instead, two more hobbits are chosen, the least and the last: the youngsters Merry and Pippin. They are chosen not for their strength or valor but simply because they insist that Frodo not leave without them. In voicing their reason for this demand, Merry utters words that, if Sauron could have heard and heeded them, would have shaken his mighty fortress at Barad-dûr to its foundations:

> "You can trust us to stick with you through thick and thin—to the bitter end," said Merry. "And you can trust us to keep any secret of yours—closer than you keep it yourself. But you cannot trust us to let you face trouble alone, and go off without a word. . . . Frodo, we are your friends."[3]

So it is with those who are tempted to cynicism in a world overwhelmed by both inward and outward violence, by the exploitation of rich and poor alike, by the commodification of almost everything, especially religion, and by the collapse of democratic civilization itself. True friendship endures when all else fails. In fact, the friendships forged amidst your devotion to the high aims and purposes of Reba Place will last even when—no: especially when—your efforts fail. Most lasting lessons are learned from losses rather than victories. And the friendships acquired in losing battles fought on behalf of the worthiest of missions, the gospel itself, are like none other. Indeed, friendship is the very basis of Christian community, for the church is an extended set of friendships—and not only among those who share the same commitments: Christian friendship must also be extended to enemies. Were it not for Frodo's repeated displays of friendship to the enemy Gollum, the final destruction of the Ring would not have happened.

3. Tolkien, *Lord of the Rings*, 103.

Communal hope also depends on communal vision. What the Fellowship of the Ring gradually discovers is that though they themselves may be defeated and their mission thus fail, good itself can never finally be vanquished. This truth is discerned, surprisingly, by Sam. As the son of a peasant farmer, Sam is the least cultured and seemingly the least reflective member of the company. He often blunders, causing more trouble than he might seem to be worth. And yet Sam undergoes the greatest moral growth of all the characters in the novel, so that by the end he is prepared to become the mayor of Hobbiton when he returns home.

Sam is also a hobbit gifted with keen metaphysical vision that is made manifest in a moment of apparent hopelessness. Near the end of their wearying journey, he and Frodo are deep within Mordor, the murderous and blighted realm occupied by Sauron himself. As they are crawling like insects on a vast slagheap, all their efforts seeming to have failed, Sam beholds a single star shimmering above the suffocating atmosphere of Mordor:

> There, peeping among the cloud-wrack above a dark tor high up in the mountains, Sam saw a white star twinkle for a while. The beauty of it smote his heart, as he looked up out of that forsaken land, and hope returned to him. For like a shaft, clear and cold, the thought pierced him that in the end the Shadow was only a small and passing thing: there was light and high beauty for ever beyond its reach. . . . Now, for a moment, his own fate, even his master's, ceased to trouble him. He crawled back into the brambles and laid himself by Frodo's side, and putting away all fear he cast himself into a deep and untroubled sleep.[4]

Sam has discerned what a community such as Reba Place must never lose: namely, a vision of the relative power of good and evil, light and dark, life and death—indeed, hope and despair. The darkened sky of Mordor, all but quenching the tiny light from this single star, would seem to signal the triumph of evil once and for all. Yet Sam has learned to have what we have heard St. Paul call hope beyond hope. He sees that the star and the shadows are not locked in a dualistic combat of equals: nor are they engaged in a battle whose outcome remains uncertain. Sam has discovered the deep and paradoxical truth that the darkness has no meaning apart from the light. The night that seeks to snuff it out is but a "small and passing thing." Light—like truth and beauty and goodness—is both the primal and the final reality. The immensely distant and seemingly insignificant

4. Ibid., 901.

star both penetrates and defines the gargantuan gloom. "The light shines in the darkness, and the darkness did not overcome it" (John 1:5).

Such a vision of the final triumph of the kingdom against which our Lord promised that not even the gates of hell shall prevail protects Christians from cynicism and gives them hope that they must measure their work not by the standards of success but always and only by faithfulness. Yet such faith is more than vision; it is also action. It is not surprising that St. Paul ties his magnificent discourse on hope, in Romans 5, to endurance. For Christian friendship and vision-inspired hope issue in endurance. In the Greco-Roman world it was called fortitude or courage, and it was displayed at its highest pitch in battle, especially in the warrior who died for his country. The masculine pronoun is appropriate here, because the ancients did not believe women to be capable of such military bravery. Christians discerned, already in the New Testament, that women are often more able to live courageous and steadfast lives. Jesus' male disciples all fled in defeat after the crucifixion, having despaired of all hope. It was the women alone who did not flee; instead, they went to visit his tomb—if not exactly in hope of his resurrection, then still in the assurance that Jesus' death had not brought his kingdom to an end.

There is only one female hero in *The Lord of the Rings*, Éowyn the shieldmaiden. Like Joan of Arc, she has to disguise herself as a man in order to enter combat. In search of heroic renown she acquits herself valiantly, slaying Angmar, the witch-king of the ringwraiths. Yet Éowyn learns that there is a gift far greater than pagan fearlessness and fame, and she learns it from Aragorn, the noble warrior with whom she has become infatuated. He tells her that worldly praise is as nothing in comparison to anonymous endurance: "A time may come soon," he says, "when none shall return [from battle]. Then there will be need of valour without renown, for none shall remember the deeds done in the last defense of your homes. Yet the deeds will not be less valiant because they are unpraised."[5] Such is the character of most of the deeds performed at Reba Place. The world pays them little if any regard, and the church but little if any more. To those of small faith, this could be cause for immense cynicism. But for those who live in true friendship, for those who share true vision of the finally triumphant kingdom, this is a paradoxical cause for hope, even for rejoicing.

Nowhere are such paradoxical hope and joy better displayed than when Sam and Frodo reach the edge of Mordor. Their hope for final success

5. Ibid., 767.

in destroying the Ring is all but gone. This is Sauron's realm, and his great roving eye is seeking them out and will surely find them. Then will they be crushed, exterminated, blotted out of all remembrance. They and their mission will have come to naught, and no one will ever know that they have fought so valiantly. Yet it is none other than Sam who finds cause for hope despite such a bleak forecast. Sam recognizes that both as individuals and communities, we all play a role within some larger story, whether for good or ill. He and Frodo have a revealing exchange about the nature of stories and thus about the quality of enduring hope:

> "I don't like anything here at all," said Frodo. . . . "Earth, air and water all seem accursed. But so our path is laid." "Yes, that's so," said Sam. "And we shouldn't be here at all, if we'd known more about it before we started. But I suppose it's often that way. The brave things in the old tales and songs. . . . Folk seem to have been just landed in them, usually—their paths were laid that way. . . . But I expect they had lots of chances, like us, of turning back, only they didn't. And if they had, we shouldn't know, because they'd be forgotten. We hear about those as just went on—and not all to a good end, mind you; at least not to what folk inside a story and not outside it call a good end. . . . Don't the great tales ever end?" "No, they never end as tales," said Frodo. "But the people in them come, and go when their part's ended. Our part will end later—or sooner."[6]

We could hardly ask for a better description of Christian hope than Sam's subgrammatical dialogue with Frodo. They both understand that they are not the captains of their destiny or masters of their fate; they are but miniscule players within a grand providential story. Insofar as they may be remembered and honored at all, it will not be because they were victorious, much less because they lived to savor their triumph. On the contrary, they may come to a disastrous end, in misery and inglorious defeat. Yet this is no cause for despair. Their hope lies in the small roles they have faithfully enacted within the cosmic drama of redemption. When their small scene is finished, others will come to take their place. And because they have advanced the Playmaker's design, if only a little, they cannot be rendered hopeless.

Our friend Stanley Hauerwas once gave excellent advice to my wife and me as we were working through a crisis with our son, Kenneth, who has schizophrenia. Having known schizophrenia close at hand, Hauerwas

6. Ibid., 697.

also knows that it is an incurable disease. He warned Suzanne and me that we must not place our hope in Kenneth's improvement—constantly nourishing the expectation that he will get better and thus that our own lives will be made easier. "If you do," said our truth-speaking friend, "hope will kill you." This is not to say that we don't pray for Kenneth and constantly seek his welfare. It is to confess, instead, that our final hope for our son must lie in Another City.

Hauerwas's hard words also apply to those who minister at Reba Place. The world may lie in moral ruin, and democracy may itself be wrecked. Yet if we put our hope in the rapid remedy of such calamities, we will indeed be killed by such worldly hope. We will end in cynicism and despair. Authentic Christian hope is found where all worldly possibility has been exhausted: where Christian faith and Christian love have nourished both personal humility and communal vision, enabling us to endure in hope to the end.

11

A Theologian in Baghdad

by Peter Dula

Here is the first paragraph of a letter that I wrote to my home church, Chapel Hill Mennonite Fellowship, from Baghdad on Easter Sunday 2004.

> Jesus has indeed risen even if it was a hell of a long time ago and even if there is no evidence of it in Baghdad. Except, perhaps, the fact that church last night was packed despite the RPGs at the nearby military base earlier in the morning. This year the Saturday vigil was from 5:30 to 7:00 instead of all night. I went with Father Yousif to Father Sahlan's church in New Baghdad. He preached about a story from St. Ephraim, who's the most important father for these churches. Ephraim said that on Holy Saturday the good thief arrived at the gates of heaven but was denied by the angel, who said, "These gates have been closed since Adam's fall." The good thief begged and pleaded, but still the angel would not let him in, and the angel demanded a sign. So the good thief took a cross from his pocket, and the angel fell to his knees in praise and unlocked the gates. Meanwhile, in the place of the dead, Adam heard footsteps and said to his companions, "Those footsteps sound familiar; I have heard them before." And indeed he had, in the garden at the dawn of creation. Nothing was said of the current developments. Unless you count Father Sahlan, at the end of the service, announcing the times

for the next day's mass and then adding, "Please go directly home. Do not linger and do not walk home in large groups."

That was Holy Week 2004, the week, one might argue, that all the stupidity of this war, or the execution of it, became impossibly hard to deny. On Palm Sunday, the day that the people of Jerusalem took to the streets to welcome a messiah they didn't comprehend any more than we do, Moqtada al-Sadr's followers took to the streets protesting the arrest of a top aid and the closing of al-Sadr's newspaper. In this week when forgiveness triumphed over vengeance, the American military unleashed an assault on Fallujah in retaliation for the deaths of four Blackwater mercenaries. Easter Sunday, I went to the NGO Emergency Working Group meeting. Statistics were coming in from Fallujah. In this week when Christ triumphed over death, 518 Iraqis were killed. Of that number 137 were women; 100 were children under twelve.

What is theology? What is it for? What does it do? What sort of hope does it cultivate, and how?

I have been trying to teach my kids in the Christian ethics class at Eastern Mennonite University that worship is political. In other words, that going to mass in Baghdad in Holy Week was a political act. It's an old idea in John Howard Yoder and Stanley Hauerwas. Unlike the argument of the Niebuhrs and others, the church doesn't have to go outside itself for a political ethic. It doesn't have to pack up some theological insights or implications and then carry them over to another sphere and apply them. We don't have to take private, in-group ideas and translate them into public language in order to be political. Worship simply is politics, with a different hope to be sure, but a politics. To get the students to understand this, I remind them that in many countries it's illegal to gather on a Sunday morning. Or I tell them how the great Cappadocian father Basil of Caesarea used to deny communion to soldiers for a year after they returned from battle, and I suggest that maybe we should do that in our churches. Or I ask them what they think would happen if some gutsy Methodist bishop would threaten to excommunicate the president who goes to war, the way John Cardinal O'Connor threatened Catholic politicians who support abortion rights.

Or I show them the film *Romero*, the scene where he walks into the church, which the army had turned into a barracks, to recover the body of Christ, kneeling before the cross, collecting the wafers while the bullets shatter the cross above him. And he returns a few moments later with the congregation and tells them, "You are the body of Christ. You, the suffering poor, gathered around this table and this cross."

I got their first papers back about a month ago, the students in my ethics class, and they weren't very good. They were so not very good that it was pretty obvious that it was my fault. As is often the case, it was a pedagogical failure not a student failure. That could be for a number of reasons. It could be that I just wasn't clear enough. Or it could be because it isn't true that worship is political, or that it's only trivially true. Or it could be that on some level—the level I was at when I wrote my church telling them there was no evidence of the resurrection on Easter in Baghdad—I don't really believe that worship is politics, and my students picked that up.

During the summer following my Easter in Baghdad, my old adviser, Stanley Hauerwas, sent me a lecture he had written, which is now in the online *Journal of Religion, Conflict, and Peace*. There he took the worship-is-politics argument and ratcheted it up a notch by arguing that worship is the church's alternative to war. The sacrifice of the Son of God replaces and overcomes the sacrifices we enact in war, the sacrifices George Bush invokes when he urges the United States to stay the course in Iraq so that thousands of American soldiers will not have died in vain. Hauerwas quoted from Augustine's *City of God*: "It is we ourselves—we, his City—who are his best, his most glorious sacrifice. The mystic symbol of this sacrifice is celebrated in our oblations, familiar to the faithful." The Eucharist, Hauerwas went on, is "the witness necessary for the world to know there is an alternative to the sacrifices of war."[1]

I had been living in Baghdad for six or seven months by that time, and I wrote him back a nasty letter. I called the argument "anemic" and wrote, "You seriously want me to tell these people, 'Yes, but have you tried worship?'" It was the argument he has honed for decades. An argument he has taught a generation of theologians and others to follow. As I put it then, it's something like, "For every problem we face—global capital, war, occupation, racism, poverty—church is the answer." That's not exactly wrong, I said. But it comes too quickly. It sort of reads like a form letter. For at least a few of the problems we face, there is only silence and tears.

A few weeks after I received the paper, the U.S. Army was in a major battle with Muqtada al-Sadr's Mahdi Army in Najaf, one of the two holiest cities in Shi'a Islam. Grand Ayatollah Ali al-Sistani was away from his Najaf home for heart surgery in London. He returned three weeks into the

1. Hauerwas, "Sacrificing the Sacrifices."

battle and in just days brought it to an end. He called on the Shi'a faithful to come to Najaf, to the Shrine of Imam Ali. Tens of thousands came, many of them on foot, for the first Friday prayers in weeks. The BBC, which for the whole time had been running some of the best footage of the war from just outside the shrine, was now showing pictures of the tear-streaked faces of soldiers from both sides kissing the bullet-ridden walls of the shrine. I sent a sheepish and apologetic e-mail to Hauerwas, saying, "Ah, so this is what you meant." Trust me when I say it pained me to admit the old man was right—again.

What is theology? What kind of difference is there between saying that humans are by nature political animals and saying they are worshiping animals? When Aristotle said that humans are political beings, he meant, according to Jonathan Lear, "not . . . that a given nature forces them to huddle together, like sheep in a storm, but that human nature is realized in the political debate and enactment of what constitutes a good life. The debate itself is one of the higher expressions of human nature."[2] Aristotle thought that politics was the most important branch of the human sciences because he understood it to be the work of creating the conditions in which humans could fulfill their nature. Or better put, it's the *work* of creating those conditions, not just the conditions themselves, that makes for the perfection and completion of human nature. Politics was the organization of the polis to direct us toward our highest end, *eudaemonia*. Augustine and Aquinas thought that theology was the queen of the sciences for the exact same reasons: it was in that polis called church that we could find the conditions to complete and perfect our nature, that is, to become Christlike, to become friends with God by being friends with each other.

In that light, it becomes possible to wonder if the politics of nation-states and global economies are really politics at all. Just insofar as they are not interested in the good, let alone negotiating goods, they're not just postdemocratic, they're postpolitical. It's no longer the politics of Jesus versus the politics of humans, or Christian politics versus pagan politics, it's the political and the nonpolitical, or the political and the antipolitical.

Under such conditions I understand Hauerwas to be asking us to throw our nets on the other side. So I could talk about 153 different hopeful things. I could talk about L'Arche communities, particularly the one I was connected to in Mosul, or the Industrial Areas Foundation and their radical-democratic community organizing, often among diverse churches,

2. Lear, *Open Minded*, 169.

synagogues and mosques. I could talk about community-bike projects around the country, like one we're starting in Harrisonburg. Or simply mention the fact that 75 percent of the community-supported agriculture projects in this country started in the last seven years—that is, since the Bush administration. So now thousands of people are finding their small ways to opt out of the global economy and create local forms of authentic politics.

But instead of talking about those things, I want to go back to Iraq. A year after Hauerwas sent me that paper, I found myself in Mosul. Mosul is the seat of the government of Ninawah, also known as Nineveh. I remind you that George Bush and Abu Musab al-Zarqawi are not the first fundamentalists who have wanted to destroy that town. It's one of the last cities to still possess the remarkable diversity of the old Middle East. Kurds, Arabs, Turkmen, Christians, Yazidis, and Mandeans all live here. It's the center of Iraqi Christianity. If you meet an Iraqi Christian in Damascus or Detroit, chances are they'll tell you that they're from Mosul.

I went there to spend three days, August 14–16, with the sisters of the Sacred Heart of Jesus, an indigenous Iraqi religious order. They run a women's shelter in Mosul that Mennonite Central Committee (MCC) was supporting, and I wanted to visit, and they asked me to come that week because August 15 is their most important feast, the Feast of the Assumption of the Blessed Virgin Mary, the day that Mary, Mother of God, was taken bodily into heaven. They venerate Mary because they know that, in Hans Urs von Balthasar's words, she "draws no line of demarcation between her uniqueness and the numberless generations. By not doing so she enters into communion with all these generations within the encompassing mercy of God, enters into an inward communion of destiny. It is a calamitous destiny."[3]

What is theology? Surely if it is anything, it is this: "I believe in God the Father almighty, Maker of heaven and earth, and in Jesus Christ, his only Son, our Lord, who was conceived of the Holy Spirit and born of the Virgin Mary." Mariology may seem like a strange topic for a Mennonite theologian. I'm taking you where the nuns took me. If we don't know what to do with Mary, it may be because we—I mean Mennonites—don't know what to do with the creed. At best we accept it grudgingly and then move on to the important stuff, like discipleship. But I know some who would argue that it is a failure of discipleship to not realize that Mary represents

3. Balthasar, *You Have Words*, 140.

discipleship here. That is, our failure to understand Mary is due to the sexism that haunts theology to its core. Mary, Rowan Williams points out, should not be read alone. She should be read alongside Pilate, the only other human being mentioned in the creed other than Jesus and herself—the one who said yes to Jesus alongside the one who said no.[4] The creed offers this teenage girl from Nazareth as the alternative to empire.

I had to beg and cajole and arm twist to get the MCC partners in Kurdistan to let me go to Mosul. August 15 was the day for the referendum on the new constitution, and such days were likely occasions for violence, good days to stay out of cities like Mosul. But since I am a theology student, I couldn't resist the opportunity for a literal enactment of worship as politics. I wanted to watch the nuns choose to celebrate the assumption of the Blessed Virgin instead of voting. These are women whose explicitly stated mission is to the least, who take them into their home and feed them and tend them when they are sick, and invite them—Christian, Muslim, Yazidi, Mandean—into their chapel three times a day to pray together. On Pilate's day in Baghdad, I wanted to be with those who had said yes, and understood that yes as a clear echo of the woman whose pregnancy made Herod shake.

In Kurdistan I was asking every Iraqi NGO staffer I met about the constitution, the draft of which was then due, after six short months of work by UN, U.S., and Iraqi technocrats in the Green Zone. The staffers were all worried about one thing: women's rights. In the van I asked Basma, Noor, and Celia, "What do you think will happen with the new constitution?" Sr. Basma said, "The what?" When she realized what I meant, she just laughed and said, "We are nuns. It's not our concern." Sr. Noor said, "Politics. Lies. *Ya haraam*."

We passed on the road dozens of posters promoting the constitution. The UN had distributed about a million of these things. Most of them read, "Our hands write it. Our hearts await it." This too provoked giggles. "It's not our hands," they said. The "our" here could mean the sisters. Or it could mean the church. Or it could simply mean ordinary folks who as usual are forgotten by the politicians.

After mass, the sisters scattered to different homes in the village. They all had relatives or friends to go to. I went with Sr. Maria and Sr. Hanaa to Maria's sister's home for an enormous breakfast of bread, meat, and *kube*, which are a sort of breaded meatballs that are traditional for the Feast of

---

4. Williams, *Tokens of Trust*, 76.

the Assumption; every home makes hundreds of them, keeps some at the house to feed the visitors all day, and takes the rest to the church. All day the poor of the village, Christian and Muslim, can come to the church to eat.

I could call that Eucharist, but they might think that was just a willful Protestant misreading. But how about this? On the afternoon of another Sunday, August 1, that same summer, I had skipped mass and was in my hotel room writing a letter to a friend when I heard the explosion, felt the building shake and quiver, and saw the plume of smoke rising to the north, above buildings I knew housed MCC friends and partners. Then another, and another, and the sky turned charcoal gray. When I resumed my letter later that night, all I knew for sure was that the Armenian church just across the street from the Middle East Council of Churches, and several others, were hit, but I didn't know which ones. The next morning I went down to the Middle East Council of Churches and discovered that Our Lady of Rescue, a very large Syrian Catholic church, was also hit. As I was leaving, I heard there was another one near Babel College, where I was teaching. I was hoping "near" meant in the neighborhood, but as it turns out it meant Peter and Paul Chaldean, the church adjacent to the seminary and across the street from the college.

I already had an appointment with the dean for that morning at eleven, so I went over early. This was by far the worst of them and the saddest thing I saw in Iraq or ever hope to see anywhere. Ten people died, about twenty were injured. There were two car bombs there, one outside the gates and one just inside. The church has a long narrow yard in front of it, about seventy-five meters from the gate to the door, where they had let some of the cars inside to park. All of those cars were burned completely black, their parts strewn across the seminary lawn. It had gone off just as people were leaving the mass. The dean was there, pale and shaking, when I arrived. So was Dawit, one of my students, looking for his aunt who had been at the church the day before but whom no one had heard from since.

Shall we call that Eucharist? A grotesque Eucharist from some Chaldean Cormac McCarthy? From some Arab Flannery O'Connor? These are our bodies, broken for nothing. This is our blood, shed for God knows what. On that trip to Mosul a year later, Sr. Maria, the mother superior of the convent, started talking about that day. She had been at a nearby church, and she hurried over to offer any aid she could. She says that all her life she has fainted at the sight of blood, but on that day she diligently picked through car parts and ash to match up scattered human limbs for burial.

On the big table facing the congregation at the old Blossom Hill Mennonite Church in Lancaster were engraved the words, "Do this in remembrance of me." Years later I learned to understand Eucharist as literal re-membering, as piecing the body of Christ back together into one. On that day in Baghdad, Sr. Maria literalized it.

Why is it a theological failure, if it is, to say, "Jesus is risen even though it was a long time ago and there is no evidence of it in Baghdad?" What is theology? Say that theology calls us to remember the eschaton, to remember that the end times are not on their way, but began at Golgotha two thousand years ago. Say that theology means negotiating the edges between celebrating the already and mourning the not-yet, and confessing that we rarely know which is which and still less know whether to mourn or celebrate that ignorance. Say that theology means wondering if the church is a two-thousand-year-old dance before the empty tomb or a two-thousand-year-old funeral at the foot of the cross. Say that doing theology means recovering a sense of the world as pervasively shot through with grace and beauty, and hoping that looks like a garden in bloom, but fearing it looks like the lawn outside Peter and Paul Chaldean Catholic Church. Say that inhabiting those tensions is called discipleship.

I began with Chapel Hill Mennonite Fellowship, so let me end with it. Their pastor, Isaac Villegas, preached a sermon last summer at the Virginia Mennonite Conference Assembly. There he preached that theology dwells in the tension in Hebrews 2:7–9:

> "You have made them for a little while lower than the angels; you have crowned them with glory and honor, subjecting all things under their feet." ... As it is, we do not yet see everything in subjection to them, but we do see Jesus, who for a little while was made lower than the angels, now crowned with glory and honor because of the suffering of death.

"But we do see Jesus," the broken and bloody body of Christ scattered across the margins of the American empire. If that is helpful, it may be because we know who Jesus is, and what his death meant, and can therefore get a handle on what senseless death means. But I doubt it. If that is helpful, I also doubt that it is because we know what senseless death means, and can therefore get a handle on what the cross meant. If theology is helpful, it is because it unveils our ignorance and makes it hurt—because it shoves us into silence.

12

Closing Prayer

by Charles (Casey) Andrews

Leader: I am the Resurrection and I am the Life, says the Lord. Those who
   have faith in me shall have life, even though they may die.

Congregation: And everyone who has life and commits to me in faith
   shall not die forever. For none of us has life all by ourselves and none
   attains self-mastery after death.

Leader: Our hope is found in God alone.

Congregation: Whether we live or die we are the Lord's possession.

Leader: Our hope is found in the holy One's covenant—

Congregation: Christ has died; Christ is risen; Christ will come again.

Leader: In the midst of life we are in death;
   from whom can we seek help?
   From you alone, O Lord,
   who by our sins are justly angered.

Congregation: Holy God, holy and mighty,
    holy and merciful Savior,
    deliver us not into the bitterness of eternal death,
    and deliver our hearts from bitter living.

Leader: Lord, you know the secrets of our hearts;
    shut not your ears to our prayers,
    but spare us, O Lord.

Congregation: Holy God, holy and mighty,
    holy and merciful Savior,
    deliver us not into the bitterness of eternal death,
    and deliver our hearts from bitter living.

Leader: O worthy and eternal Judge, more just than the justice that we crave,
    do not let the pains of death turn us away from you at our last hour.

All: Holy God, holy and mighty,
    holy and merciful Savior,
    deliver us not into the bitterness of eternal death,
    and deliver our hearts from bitter living.

Leader: The Lord be with you.

Congregation: And also with you.

Leader: Let us pray: This weekend we have gathered to learn, to love, to grow, and to unburden. We believe in your power and the life that you bring. But too often we fail to see your working. We yearn to trust in your green pastures and long to hear your footfalls beside us. Instead, we dwell in the valley of death's shadow and hear the shrieks of the afflicted. We cry out.

Congregation: Please Lord, hear our prayer.

Leader: We want bread for the world and know that yours is the bread of life. But we see so many gaping mouths that cannot chew because of a lifetime of gnashing teeth. Save us from toothless hunger and toothless policies. We cry out.

Congregation: Lord, hear our prayer.

Leader: We long to be the voice of one crying out in the wilderness, the voice that speaks into the wordless place and names the unnamable. But the voice in the wilderness is the voice in Ramah, the wailing and loud lamentation of Rachel weeping for her children, refusing to be consoled because they are no more. Give ear to Rachel! We cry out.

Congregation: Lord, hear our prayer.

Leader: You have called your church to live today as all people will live someday under your reign. We have chosen instead to become mega-churches and atrophied churches. We build great monuments to make a name for ourselves upon the earth, and we press close to each other to breed community for its own sake. Open our hearts, our eyes, and our lives. Scatter us with your mighty hand to live beside all peoples, that our community may be your handiwork and our peoplehood yours alone. We cry out.

Congregation: Lord, hear our prayer.

Leader: Remember the powerless; forget not their pain.
[Names of the powerless may be spoken aloud or silently.]

Leader: Restrain the powerful, that their ambition shall not annihilate.
[Names of the powerful may be spoken aloud or silently.]

Leader: Our God in heaven,

Congregation: Hallowed be your name.
    May your kingdom come.

Leader: This is no idle plea, no hollow refrain.
    Only in your kingdom is there peace.
    Prepare us for the consequences of your kingdom.

Congregation: Thy will be done on earth—as it is in heaven.

Leader: Give all today enough to eat, and teach us to share.

Congregation: We repent of our hunger for food that comes without hunger for justice.

Leader: Make us able to forgive all oppressors, and forgive us our complicity in their oppression.

Congregation: Lord have mercy.

Leader: Lead us not into temptation.

Congregation: Let not our cynicism become paralysis. Let not our hope become ignorance.

Leader: Deliver us from this time of trial.

Congregation: For yours is the kingdom, the power, and the glory, now and forever.

All: Amen.

13

Ingredients

by Ruth Goring

Carbonated water, high fructose
corn syrup, sucrose,
caramel color, phosphoric acid,
natural flavors (vegetable source),
caffeine. One has been omitted
from the list on every can:
blood.

I am so weary of this world
and its ingredients,
its brownfields and its goldmines,
buckling bridges, planes
that strike tall buildings and explode,
open a mouth that screams,
gulps thousands to an ignited belly.

I could say no to this world,
to my own skin and language
for being tools of conquest,
desire's deformation:
hamburgers in Japan, oil wells
on paths of Alaska's caribou,
Avon sales in Brazilian jungle towns,
Coca-Cola everywhere
more fiercely craved than wine
and everywhere tainted with blood.

I could say no. I am tired
of the empire of petroleum
with its poisoned air, its gridlock,
its plastic that chokes oceans,
its long cunning violence,
its oracles of terrorism
and God on our side.
I am tired of the empire.
I am tired of listing the ingredients
and being forced to drink.
I am tired of I.

Speak a new list, my sisters,
let us write it on our hearts.
Say it is old, my brothers,
say it can become our DNA,
our blood.
Tell me what Jesus says.

Jesus says grass,
chlorophyll
and lilies of the field,
Jesus says worms
that swarm in backyard compost
or kitchen vermiculture.
Stay awake,
you will have trouble in this world,
Jesus says we,
Jesus says sing.
Get in the way,
on earth as it is in heaven.
Jesus says caribou, sparrows,
ceiba trees, mustard seeds.
Jesus says hands,
apples, loaves and fishes,
wine.

Jesus says blood—his own.
Jesus says flesh, God's dwelling,
God's scars.

Jesus says Rogers Park and Eritrea,
Colombia, Queens, South Central,
Michoacán, Cambodia, Burma,
Arctic village, Egypt, Tanzania,
Iran, Baghdad, St. Petersburg, India,
Trinidad and Tobago, Plow Creek Farm,
far as the curse is found.

Jesus says come to me,
all who are tired and burdened.
Fish, lit coals, a bit of salt:
I've made you breakfast on the shore.
Say yes.

Bibliography

Aristotle. *The Nicomachean Ethics*. New York: Oxford University Press, 1998.

Badiou, Alain. *Ethics: An Essay on the Understanding of Evil*. Translated by Peter Hallward. London: Verso, 2001.

Balthasar, Hans Urs von. *You Have Words of Eternal Life: Scripture Meditations*. San Francisco: Ignatius, 1991.

Berry, Wendell. *What Are People For? Essays*. New York: North Point, 1990.

Born, Daniel. *The Birth of Liberal Guilt in the English Novel: Charles Dickens to H. G. Wells*. Chapel Hill: University of North Carolina Press, 1995.

Brink, Lindsey. *The Age of Abundance: How Prosperity Transformed America's Politics and Culture*. New York: Collins, 2007.

Campbell, Will D. *Brother to a Dragonfly*. New York: Continuum, 2000.

Chesterton, G. K. *Robert Browning*. Whitefish, MT: Kessinger, 2003.

——. *The Uses of Diversity: A Book of Essays*. New York: Dodd, Mead, and Company, 1921.

Dostoevsky, Fyodor. *The Brothers Karamazov*. New York: Farrar, Straus and Giroux, 2002 [1880].

Fainaru, Steve, and Anthony Shadid. "Kurdish Officials Sanction Abductions in Kirkuk; U.S. Memo Says Arabs, Turkmens Secretly Sent to the North." *Washington Post*, June 15, 2005.

Girard, René. *Things Hidden since the Foundation of the World*. Translated by Stephen Bann and Michael Metteer. Palo Alto: Stanford University Press, 1987.

Goodchild, Philip. "Capital and Kingdom: An Eschatological Ontology." In *Theology and the Political: The New Debate*, edited by Creston Davis, John Milbank and Slavoj Zizek. Durham: Duke University Press, 2005.

Hartley, Benjamin. "Holiness Evangelical Urban Mission and Identity in Boston, 1860–1910." ThD diss., Boston University, 2005.

Hauweras, Stanley. "Sacrificing the Sacrifices of War." *Journal of Religion, Conflict, and Peace* (Fall 2007). Online: http://www.plowsharesproject.org/journal.

Hedemann, Ed, and Ruth Benn, editors. *War Tax Resistance: A Guide to Withholding Your Support from the Military*. New York: War Resisters League, 2003.

Bibliography

Jordan, Clarence. *The Cotton Patch Gospel: Matthew and John.* Macon, GA: Smyth & Helwys, 2004.

Jordan, June. *Some of Us Did Not Die: New and Selected Essays.* New York: Basic Civitas, 2002.

King, Martin Luther, Jr. "The Case against Tokenism: Address delivered on 7/19/62." *New York Times Magazine,* August 5, 1962.

———. "Letter from Birmingham Jail." *Christian Century,* June 12, 1963.

———. "My Pilgrimage to Nonviolence." *Fellowship* 24 (1958).

———. *Stride toward Freedom: The Montgomery Story.* New York: Harper & Brothers, 1958.

———. "Three Ways of Meeting Oppression." In *Between Worlds: A Reader, Rhetoric, and Handbook,* 5th edition, edited by Susan Bachmann and Melinda Barth. New York: Longman, 2006.

———. *The Trumpet of Conscience.* New York: Harper & Row, 1968.

———. "Where Do We Go from Here?" Annual report delivered at the 11th convention of the Southern Christian Leadership Conference, August 16, 1967, Atlanta, Georgia.

Lear, Jonathan. *Open Minded: Working Out the Logic of the Soul.* Cambridge: Harvard University Press, 1998.

———. *Radical Hope: Ethics in the Face of Cultural Devastation.* Cambridge: Harvard University Press, 2006.

Lee, Dallas. *The Cotton Patch Evidence: The Story of Clarence Jordan and the Koinonia Farm Experiment (1942–1970).* Americus, GA: Koinonia Partners, 1971.

Lull, Timothy F., editor. *Martin Luther's Basic Theological Writings,* 2nd edition. Minneapolis: Fortress, 2005.

Luther, Martin. *Commentary on Galatians.* Grand Rapids: Kregel, 1987.

Marcel, Gabriel. *The Mystery of Being, vol. 2: Faith and Reality.* Chicago: St. Augustine's, 2001.

Marsh, Charles. *The Beloved Community: How Faith Shapes Social Justice from the Civil Rights Movement to Today.* New York: Basic, 2004.

Marx, Anthony W. *Faith in Nation: Exclusionary Origins of Nationalism.* New York: Oxford University Press, 2005.

McWhorter, Diane. "The N-Word: Unmentionable Lessons of the Midterm Aftermath." *Slate,* November 28, 2006. Online: http://www.slate.com/id/2154567.

Moltmann, Jürgen. "Meditation über die Hoffnung." In *Die Quelle des Lebens.* Gütersloh: Kaiser, 1997.

Nafziger, Tim. "Cynicism, Hope, Discipleship, Democracy." *God's Politics* blog, September 2007. Online: http://blog.beliefnet.com/godspolitics/2007/09/cynicism-hope-discipleship-and.html.

Nietzsche, Friedrich. *On the Genealogy of Morals and Ecce Homo.* Edited by Walter Kaufmann. New York: Vintage, 1989 [1887].

O'Connor, Flannery. *Everything That Rises Must Converge.* New York: Farrar, Straus and Giroux, 1965.

Perelman, Michael. *The Invention of Capitalism: Classical Political Economy and the Secret History of Primitive Accumulation.* Durham: Duke University Press, 2000.

Schumpeter, Joseph A. *Capitalism, Socialism, and Democracy.* New York: Routledge, 2006 [1942].

Sobrino, Jon. *Fuera de los pobres no hay salvación. Pequeños ensayos utópico-proféticos.* Madrid: Trotta, 2007.

Bibliography

Steuart, James. *An Inquiry into the Principles of Political Economy, Being an Essay on the Science of Domestic Policy in Free Nations.* London: A. Millar and T. Cadell, 1805.

Taylor, Charles. "A Different Kind of Courage." Review of *Radical Hope: Ethics in the Face of Cultural Devastation,* by Jonathan Lear. *New York Review of Books* 54:7 (2007).

This American Life. "My Big Break, Act Two: What Happens in Baghdad, Stays in Baghdad." January 20, 2006. Online: http://www.thislife.org/Radio_Episode.aspx?sched=1116.

Tolkien, J. R. R. *The Lord of the Rings,* single-volume edition. New York: Houghton Mifflin, 1994.

Wallis, Jim. "Idols Closer to Home: Radical Christian Substitutes for Grace." *Sojourners* 8:5 (1979).

Weatherford, Jack. *The History of Money.* New York: Three Rivers, 1998.

Wheelan, Charles. *Naked Economics: Undressing the Dismal Science.* New York: Norton, 2003.

White, Curtis. "The New Censorship." *Harper's Magazine* (August 2003).

Williams, Rowan. "Introduction." In *Theology and the Political: The New Debate,* edited by Creston Davis, John Milbank and Slavoj Zizek. Durham: Duke University Press, 2005.

———. *Tokens of Trust: An Introduction to Christian Belief.* Louisville, KY: Westminster John Knox, 2007.

Contributors

Charles (Casey) Andrews is an assistant professor of English at Whitworth University in Spokane, Washington. He was a visiting assistant professor of humanities and English at Valparaiso University while on the Cynicism and Hope planning committee. The closing prayer was created in conversation with Katie Dahlaw of Living Water Community Church.

Nancy Elizabeth Bedford is Georgia Harkness Professor of Applied Theology at Garrett-Evangelical Theological Seminary in Evanston, Illinois; a nonresident professor at the ISEDET Institute in Buenos Aires; and a member of Reba Place Church. Her latest book is *La porfía de la resurrección: Ensayos desde el feminismo teológico latinoamericano* (The stubbornness of the resurrection: Essays in Latin American theological feminism), forthcoming from FTL/RDC in Buenos Aires.

Gregory A. Clark is a professor of philosophy at North Park University. He and his wife, Heather, have been part of the Reba Place Fellowship intentional community since 1994.

Meg E. Cox is a freelance writer and editor and is on the staff of the *Christian Century*. She is a member of Living Water Community Church.

Bren Dubay is the director of Koinonia Farm, an intentional Christian community in Americus, Georgia. Before moving to Koinonia, Dubay was a faculty member, spiritual director, and writer-in-residence at St. Catherine's Montessori School. She has also been playwright-in-residence at Rice University in Houston, Texas, and has a background in community service, church history, and management.

CONTRIBUTORS

Peter Dula is assistant professor of religion and culture at Eastern Mennonite University. He was the Iraq program coordinator for Mennonite Central Committee from 2004 to 2006.

Thomas Finger is an independent scholar who is engaged in ecumenical and interfaith work with the Mennonite Church USA, Mennonite World Conference, and Mennonite Central Committee.

Ruth Goring's poems have been published in her collection *Yellow Doors* (WordFarm, 2004) and in journals such as *Mars Hill Review, Conte, Out of Line, Raving Dove, Target Earth,* and *The Externalist.* She is an editor at a major academic press and along with her husband, Daniel de la Pava, codirects Across the Americas (www.acrosstheamericas.org).

Ric Hudgens is the lead pastor of Reba Place Church and a student at the University of Chicago Divinity School.

D. Stephen Long is a professor of systematic theology at Marquette University in Milwaukee. He thanks Geoff Holsclaw for assistance with his essay.

Tim Nafziger is a Mennonite, Web developer, activist, and writer. He helped found the Young Anabaptist Radicals blog (at young.anabaptistradicals.org), is a regular blogger for the *Mennonite* magazine, and serves as outreach coordinator for Christian Peacemaker Teams. He is an enthusiastic member of Living Water Community Church.

Dale Suderman was a therapist at the Salvation Army Community Sanctions Center in Chicago. He graduated from Tabor College in Hillsboro, Kansas, and Associated Mennonite Biblical Seminary. Dale wrote a bimonthly newspaper column called "View from Afar" for his hometown paper in Kansas and occasionally reviewed books for the *Common Review.* In spring 2008 Dale suffered a stroke, and he is now in recovery.

Ralph C. Wood is University Professor of Theology and Literature at Baylor University in Waco, Texas.